Michael Barratt

by

Michael Barratt

WOLFE PUBLISHING LIMITED
10 EARLHAM STREET
LONDON WC2H 9LP

Printed in Great Britain by

THE STELLAR PRESS HATFIELD HERTS

Contents

Preface

FROM MACLUHAN to MacNeil, Bakewell to Baker, Day and night, the library of television grows apace. This book makes no attempt to analyse the medium as those others have done. (Indeed, my friend Robert MacNeil will probably be appalled by the personalised approach of the following pages.)

My motives for writing are various. Most of my work in television – give or take an occasional film – is as fleetingly impermanent as the tick of a second on the studio clock. Often, that is just as well. But it does leave a yearning for the more lasting qualities of a book's hard covers.

Then again, daily work in front of the cameras requires the development of a peculiar kind of memory, an artificial mental mechanism. In my experience, an ability to digest and store words, names, and background information at high speed for a programme demands an equal ability to clear the mind by discarding yesterday's facts and figures. The consequence is that I am frustratingly unable to recall even historic events in which I have been concerned and the discipline of recording them on paper is a necessary one.

In place of memory, for the writing of this book, I have delved deeply into the BBC's transcript files and I am grateful to the Corporation for its assistance.

A third motive is that television reporting invariably and inevitably leaves gaps in any story. In the studio, time runs out and the high point of an interview all too often comes in the hospitality room after the programme; in film stories, as every reporter will tell you, the real gems of a commentary are lost on the cutting room floor. So this is an opportunity to fill in some of those gaps.

A reporter's job is an apparently contradictory one: to immerse himself as deeply as possible in a story – and then to stand back from it to give an 'objective' assessment. My own objectivity has been called in question countless times. Yet my mind has certainly been sufficiently open for my opinions and attitudes to alter under the influence of people I have met and places I have seen in the course of work – before and since I took a nervous step into the world of television.

I hope that will become apparent.

CHAPTER ONE

Will the
Real Michael Barratt...

'KNOW THYSELF', said the Oracle, and perhaps it is time that I tried to.

My name you know. My age is 45. My wife's name is Joan, our children's Mark, Andrew, Eve, Paul, Jane and Rachel.

We live in a large Victorian house in 11 acres of rural royal Berkshire along with 180 hens, 90 turkeys, a West Highland White Terrier, countless cats and my pet white Mercedes car.

Not much clue to character in those basic statistics – unless you deduce that I am oversexed and overpaid.

Mrs V. McF, however, knows me much more intimately. She is an arthritic old lady who writes to me every Sunday without fail to tell me what a patently charming fellow I am, a gentle man, a lover of people whose warm smile keeps her going through the long days and nights of her lonely late years. Every letter is simply initialled, without an address, and carries a shaky drawing of a waste paper basket with an apology for taking up my time.

Other viewers claim greater insight. They see me as a rude and aggressive fellow who carries arrogant Yorkshire bluntness to irritating extremes. I am either a typical Commie fellow-traveller (which means I asked dear Mr Heath a tricky question) or a dyed-in-the-wool Tory plutocrat (which means I had a sceptical attitude to a wildcat striker). In any case, I should be banned from a medium which can so greatly influence people. Those kind of letters, oddly, are often written in green ink.

Who are they all talking about? Me – or some puppet who

All right, it's me!

exhibits my face and my name on the screen? It is depressingly difficult to know myself.

Certainly curiosity has always been with me. At school, as far back as I can remember, I was asking questions about the small world in which I lived and reporting the answers in a hand-produced tabloid newspaper.

Naturally, too, at the age of nine, when my mother died, there were deeply needed answers to be sought about life and death itself. 'Mummy has gone on a long journey' didn't begin to be a satisfactory explanation though perhaps it ought to have been.

The puzzling paradox then, as now, was that my curiosity was deeply introverted and I suffered from the most painful shyness, yet I had a compulsive need to air my questions in public and indeed to parade my non-existent but longed-for talent to entertain other people.

Thus, at school, I produced that newspaper and strutted on the stage in plays and concerts, yet I could not for the life of me raise my hand in class or ask to 'leave the room' because the attention it brought would make me blush scarlet. There's a riddle for you amateur psychiatrists.

I remember in desperation replying to an advertisement in the 'Wizard' which offered the chance to 'CURE BLUSHING — FREE!' A few days later there arrived in the post one of those 'plain envelopes' which the headmaster decided to investigate.

He called me into his study and made me open it in his presence. Out tumbled 'free' literature which explained how, for £5 or so, I could embark on a course to cure my embarrassing complaint. I have never blushed quite such a deep red as at that moment.

This shyness even complicated my home life. Thus, at the age of 16 when I secured my Higher Leaving Certificate in Greek, Latin, English, History and Maths, my father – a civil servant of awesome integrity and unbounded ambition for his two sons – planned my progress through university into some professional career that would culminate in my being Prime Minister. For agonising weeks I could not bring myself to tell him that I did not want to go to university, that I wanted to start work there and then in a newspaper.

What made my ultimate confession harder was that there was no evidence of any kind that I had a chance of success in journalism. I had no friends or relatives in that line, nor had I ever been inside a newspaper office. Goodness knows why, but I knew I had to do it.

It was in 1944, with the war still on, that I went for an interview for the exalted post of office boy with the *Sunday Mail* in Glasgow. The editor then was Clem Livingstone, one of the most brilliant newspapermen Scotland has ever produced.

Clem was, not surprisingly, dubious. He told me to go away, learn to type and to secure a certificate for at least 120 words a minute in shorthand. So I enrolled at a business college in the city, a lone lad sitting at the back of classes full of girls. Again I was the thoroughly embarrassed odd man out – a fact

WHERE ARE THEY NOW?

Rossall, 1941. This group picture of the Junior School shows many well-remembered faces but long-forgotten names. No doubt many of them are today pillars of our society, though I never come across them. That's me on the extreme left of the row of senior citizens. My brother Roger is fifth from the left on the top row. He's in Australia now, father of five and a prosperous farmer – the result of sheer hard work as a farm manager in this country and the guts to make the most of the 'land of opportunity'. According to him, I'm a wingeing Pom!

which probably spurred me to get that certificate in ten weeks flat.

It was while I was at the college that a teacher reprimanded me for crossing out mistakes in my exercise pad. 'You must keep the page neat', she said, 'and rub out any errors.' I explained I had no rubber and was dispatched across the road to a newsagent's to buy one.

'Have you any rubbers?' I asked the man.

'Yes, sir', he said. 'Two-and-six, three-and-six and washable.'

Blushing Barratt fled.

My qualifications then for entering journalism were twofold. Firstly, I had learnt shorthand. Secondly, my ambition to be a reporter was so strong that there was nothing else I would have remotely considered doing. I would have gladly travelled to the ends of the earth to find a job as a tea boy in a newspaper office.

'News sense' was not something one could learn at any university. 'Ink in the veins' was a corny cliché – unless you had it. In many eyes these vague phrases constituted no sort of qualification to enter a profession and the demand grew, within and without the industry, for some system of entry which demanded visible academic achievement.

When that view won the day, the decline of journalistic standards began. The door was closed to the great romantics who had traditionally made the best reporters, columnists, sub-editors. They were repelled by a formalised scheme which demanded A levels, or university degrees, or proficiency certificates or whatever, in the manner of banking or the law or medicine.

In recent years I have many times been the victim of the new-style reporter bereft of shorthand or any grounding in the collection and assimilation of fact. He misquotes what I tell him, almost certainly misspells my name and has a careless disregard of truth, which is adapted to colour a 'clever' piece of writing.

Television critics are among the worst offenders, rarely taking the trouble to discover the background to a programme or an item which they are 'analysing'. I have even known lengthy, pseudo-intellectual critiques of film reports or inter-

WHERE ARE THEY NOW?

Outside St. Stephen's entrance to the Houses of Parliament – a group of provincial newspapermen. (Could they be anything else in that 'uniform'?). We had come from Glasgow, Cardiff, Manchester, Newcastle, Middlesbrough, Sheffield and other local paper centres for a week-long course as part of the Kemsley Newspapers training scheme in the late Forties. A valuable (if faintly paternal) scheme it was, too – and in my view preferable to the more academic and formalised training that today's reporters and sub-editors are required to undergo.

I wonder how many of this group, of which I was the baby, are now Fleet Street's household names. . . .

Topix

views carelessly ascribed to the wrong programme or even the wrong channel.

One of my earliest experiences of the Sunday paper critics followed an interview I had conducted for *Panorama* which received a highly laudatory reaction. It was, he said, 'one of the best things Michael Charlton has done so far'. In my early days, a cub reporter would have been sacked for less.

I started at thirty bob a week and wasn't allowed near a typewriter. My main jobs were to fetch the staff tea and cigarettes from the canteen and to take news copy to the government information department through which in those days newspapers operated a voluntary censorship.

If that hardly sounds like training, let me explain that running messages took me through the caseroom, the process department, the Creed room, the Presses and so on. Observing how a paper was put together gave me a head start when it came to subbing and laying out pages myself.

My first big break was to be allowed to type out the radio programmes from the *Radio Times*, from which I took the great leap forward: I was given responsibility for the horoscope.

There were two clearly defined rules about writing 'what the stars foretell'. Never predict anything precise enough to be proved inaccurate later; and always give 'healthy' advice.

Thus, 'the week ahead looks promising for Capricorns and there may well be surprises on Thursday. However, you may be tempted to extravagance in money matters and would be well advised to resist'.

In the next few years that I spent with Kemsley Newspapers in Glasgow, I experienced practically every job in the business from reporter to sub-editor, showbiz columnist to news copy-taster.

At 18 I was chief sub on the sports desk of the Sunday paper, responsible for seven 'slip' pages being put to bed every Saturday night and for giving instructions to a team of subs most of whom were twice my age. That was my first taste of a social and political dilemma which remains with me to this day. Let me explain.

Kemsley House, Glasgow, like most newspaper offices, was a closed shop. To be able to work there it was necessary to be

The theatre always had an attraction for me: When I was 16, I decided that if there were no signs of my making progress in journalism, I'd abandon the profession and try my luck on the stage. In the meantime, I spent many of my evenings with amateur companies in Glasgow, notably the New Vic, produced by that veteran of radio in Scotland, Howard Lockhart. Among the parts I played was that of Robin in Priestley's 'Time and the Conways'.

a member of the National Union of Journalists or of the Institute of Journalists. I joined the NUJ.

I had no idealistic feelings about the Union movement, for or against it. If pressed, I'd probably have expressed the non-committal opinion that it seemed 'a good thing', though it did seem strange to me that the leading lights in our particular Chapel (that's the NUJ word for an office unit) were the very men who would have lost their jobs if the management had been able to sack incompetent men with impunity.

There was, of course, a negotiated basic minimum wage. That's to say, the unions called it a minimum; the management regarded it as a maximum which they were hard pressed to pay. The full rate, however, did not apply until the age of 24. Those of us younger than that were paid the agreed rate for our age.

Thus it was that I found myself at 18 doing a senior and skilled job yet being paid no more than £3 15s. a week – something like a third of what the sports subs under me were paid for a few hours' overtime on a Saturday night. It seemed then, as it does still, grossly unfair, yet who was to blame? Should the cumbersome forces of the union have been called up to fight for an unknown lad in Glasgow? Should the bosses have been less rigid, more philanthropic by paying me more than hard-fought negotiations made them pay?

Whatever the answers, there developed in me so early in my career a determination to be independent of both sides. To blazes with the unions *and* the bosses: I set out to build a career in which I would be paid my market value. And nowadays, if I'm chairing a televised argument between management and men, you may be sure that I'm on nobody's side.

There was another little incident in those early newspaper days which has stayed, nagging, in my mind ever since. It was when I moved to the *Daily Record* (in the same office) on the news desk. As a youngster I was entrusted at first only with the unimportant little stories, tucked away at the bottom of inside pages. I yearned to be given the big story.

One night there came a Reuter's tape about an avalanche in the Alps. It was feared there might be several injured. The story was handed to me for the first edition – the usual single paragraph with a ten-point (that's pretty small) headline.

By the second edition, the story had grown. Now there were reports of people being killed and I was instructed to develop the report with a bigger headline. Later still, with mounting excitement, I turned it into an inside page lead. It had become a major disaster. I knew there was a chance that by the last edition it would be the 'splash' on the front page. I hoped that the news would get worse and I hoped so hard that I would be allowed to continue handling it.

I was. Exultant – this was, after all, a great opportunity for me to prove my worth as a sub-editor – I scrawled out the headline instructions: '60 point Gothic caps across page, WHITE DEATH HORROR'.

I left the office clutching a bundle of papers. All my own work and I knew that it was a good professional job, that front page story. On the early morning bus going back to my digs I watched people reading it. I wanted to tap them on the shoulder and say: 'I did that!'

It is, of course, arguable – indeed, I like to think it is wholly true – that my exultation that night was in every sense due to professionalism. I wanted the chance to do a highly responsible job and I wanted to prove that I could accomplish it with journalistic skill. There is nothing macabre about that.

And yet, the thought returns to me even now . . . *I wanted those people to die.*

CHAPTER TWO

The African Experience

AFRICA WILL LOOM large in these pages. I lived and worked there. Our eldest daughter was born there. I was in jail there. I lost all my possessions there. I made my first radio broadcast there. I found out about Reverence for Life there at the feet of the Master. I fell in love there – with Africa, that is – a kind of addictive love that has stricken many a man before and since.

Journalism took me from Glasgow to Leicestershire, where I was Sports Editor of the *Loughborough Monitor* and where I married Joan (poor girl) from the rival and now defunct *Leicester Evening Mail*.

Our first home was a bedsitter. Then we moved to Bradford and took an unfurnished flat. As we had no money and no possessions, we slept on the floor. In the daytime we rolled up the bedding to sit on and ate off an orange box. My favourite meal was a tin of kidney soup with potatoes, which was the best we could afford on pay days after paying back the money I had borrowed from colleagues the week before. I was a totally irresponsible young man, except in my work to which I was devoted.

I had left the mainstream of newspapers to join Watmoughs Ltd, printers and publishers of *Idle* – my office was right opposite the Idle Working Men's Club.

It was (and is) a generous firm which paid me well and moved us into a modern semi-detached house on the edge of Baildon Moor. Our first son, Mark, was born there and I began for the first time in my life to develop a sense of responsibility. The work consisted of editing the weekly *Dog World* and the monthly *Field Sports*. Other publications included *Fur and Feather* and *Racing Pigeon*.

An incompetent amateur handling an inefficient microphone . . . Over 20 years ago, as Sports Editor of the 'Loughborough Monitor', I tried my hand at soccer commentaries for the local hospital radio service. I was an abysmal failure and I think I still would be today.

They were happy days, marred only by my growing desire to be back 'where it was all happening' in daily journalism. Clearly, however, it was no springboard to Fleet Street. The Editor of the *Guardian* would hardly be impressed by my subbing of the bulldog breed notes or my reporting of the Colne and Nelson limited dog show.

The only way I could see back into newspapers was a circuitous one, so I applied for and was given the job of Assistant Editor of the *Nigerian Citizen* in Zaria, Northern Nigeria. It proved to be not only an exciting challenge – to produce a newspaper with an entirely African staff was far from easy – but also the doorway to undreamed-of opportunity and an important lesson in life.

In those days – it was 1956 when we went out there – Northern Nigeria was moving through a period of 'indirect rule' to a form of 'regional independence' under its Premier, Sir Ahmadu Bello, Sardauna of Sokoto (who was later most violently to be murdered).

'Indirect rule' applied to the *Citizen*, too. Thus the Editor was an African, Malam Cindo. On paper, I was his assistant. In fact, he would arrive in the office each morning and, like the rest of the staff, ask me what he had to do – politically, and in spheres such as ours it always seemed to me a good system, smoothing the path to self-determination. Thus, independence would mean that Cindo carried on as Editor – but did so in fact as well as in name – and that he had several years' fundamental training for the job.

The real boss at that time was another journalist from the United Kingdom, Charles Sharp, who had the title of Managing Editor, but for much of my time there he was away on leave and so the running of the paper was left to me. From the start, I had to determine my attitude to the African staff, an attitude that had to stand up to more than intellectual scrutiny because it was practically put to the test in the day-to-day business of producing a newspaper.

It was my first important experience of working side by side with black people and of course it greatly influenced my approach to race relations in later years.

White expatriates in Nigeria, as in other British colonies, fell

April 14, 1952. Joan Francesca Warner marries a 24-year-old local paper reporter with no prospects, not a bean in the bank and a single suit to his name. If only she'd known the traumas in store for her (not to mention bearing six of his children) no doubt it would have taken the smile off her face.

roughly into two distinct categories. There were those who believed in treating the Africans on a strictly master-servant relationship which lacked any trust: 'They have smaller brains than we have, they are by nature corrupt, and the only thing they understand is the big stick.'

And there were the 'liberals' who paid lip service to the 'They're-human-beings-like-the-rest-of-us' school but who, in my view, demeaned the Africans even more than the traditional colonialists by 'making allowances' for them.

I decided that the only reasonable way to run the paper was to do so exactly as I would have done back home. If a reporter, be he Hausa, Ibo, Yoruba or Tiv, was late for work in the morning, he would be reprimanded in exactly the same way as any staff man at home; an African whose output did not match up to the fairly high journalistic standards we set would be given a warning and, if there were no improvement, sacked; all the staff were trained in their various roles and then given full responsibility to get on with the job. That way, I gave them the respect of believing that they had as much ability as any journalist, black or white, anywhere.

That approach paid handsome dividends and I enjoyed my stint on the *Citizen*, although it had its special problems. One was that the staff were writing in their second language in which they were not always wholly conversant. (We had a sister paper, which cost twopence, called *Gaskiya Ta Fi Kwabo*, which was Hausa for 'Truth is Worth More than a Penny'). Subbing copy from some of our freelance contributors often tended to be an exercise in clairvoyance. How, for instance, would you have re-written this gem?

A very disgraceful occasion marked the anniversary of the UDU Zaria branch which came off on Saturday the 18th instant. Food were set up at tables when an uncultured and senseless widow entered who caused the tumult.

The widow, yet in her mourning period and with mourning garments in her body grew anxious of sexual intercourse and consequently mated with a foolish man and became under state irrespectable of her recent misfortune. This was absolutely abominable and as such she was considered un-

The oddest difficulty of all in producing the *Citizen* was to be found in the composing room. The type was set in Mono – that's to say, it was composed by hand, letter by letter – and assembled in the usual forme, with rules to divide the columns. Painstaking, but straightforward enough – except for the fact that those Africans were incapable of differentiating a straight line from a crooked one. It's a disability I have never seen mentioned elsewhere.

The result was that when the formes of type were locked up and ready for printing, the columns would look for all the world like stretches of the Serpentine. I would point this out to the man who had made up the page and his face would be pained with perplexity: he did not understand what I was talking about. He would examine the page of type minutely and see nothing wrong with it.

'But surely, Ibrahim, you can see that those column rules are not straight?'

'No, sir, I'm sorry.' But he would have another go – and this time the columns would twist and turn in slightly different directions. This meant, among other things, that the type was not firmly held in the forme and when it was transferred to a trolley to go to the Press room, it would all fall out – a great heap of thousands of metal letters on the floor.

The editorial content of the paper was the subject of a constant battle, not with the Africans but with our white expatriate colleagues in Kaduna, the capital, who ran the government information service.

Although our aim was that the *Citizen* should be seen to be

WHERE ARE THEY NOW?

This was the staff of the 'Nigerian Citizen' in Zaria, Northern Nigeria, in 1956. A happy mixture of Hausas, Yorubas, Ibos and several other tribes, some of them to be turned into bitter enemies and torn apart in the Civil War. Some of them, I know, went back to their farms during the war, preferring to hack a meagre living out of the hard earth rather than becoming embroiled in the conflict. Perhaps some of them died. Perhaps some of them killed each other . . . In the centre of the front row is Malam Cindo, then the 'Citizen's' Editor. On his right, Managing Editor – now Director of Scarborough and District Newspapers – Charles Sharp.

truly independent in those exciting days of political change, we were dependent for much of our income on the regional government who felt that we should toe the line by printing, without comment or alteration, their official handouts. We for our part were determined when necessary to bite the hand that fed us and I constantly lectured the editorial staff on the need to question and check government 'information' just as they would the contributions from any other outside source.

Notably, it was the British and not the Nigerians in the regional administration who were always objecting to our independent line, often threatening the withdrawal of funds if we did not toe their line. Men like the Premier, who needed our support, would be much more tolerant and understanding of our attitude.

Much the same was true of my weekly political broadcasts which (though I could not know it then) were to become the first step on my own road to current affairs television.

In Kaduna, a young colonial officer by the name of John Wilkinson was in charge of the Northern output of Nigerian Broadcasting. With considerable courage, he asked me to provide a weekly commentary on political developments in the Northern Region. I was free to criticise or praise as I saw fit – and remember, with the wind of change blowing hard in the country then, the political atmosphere was decidedly unsettled.

John took two great gambles, the first with me because I had never broadcast before, the second with his own career because he was breaking the rules by introducing comment into the NBC's output of current affairs programmes.

His gamble paid off. (He later became, incidentally, Head of the African Service of the BBC back in London). For me, it was an exciting new challenge that was to change my life. I became deeply involved in and engrossed by the emergence of this great nation of so many tribes and by the form of its attaining independence.

How were the great traditions of British parliamentary democracy to be adapted to this vast country of different tongues, different religions, different ways of life? How could the best of Westminster be grafted on to what was best of the traditional ways of these tribes and races? What did we mean by 'best' anyway? Best for whom?

The Moslem Fulani rule of the North had been achieved by conquest – the Jehad, or Holy War – and had been maintained by what seemed to the British an archaic feudal administration largely based on corruption and religious fear. But these were appalling over-simplifications.

I found that there was a great deal to admire, and to learn from, the Nigerian way of life. At its very roots there was a great strength stemming from the family unit. Thus, social 'problems' such as we were most accustomed to, like unemployment, did not exist – at least, not in the same form. A man out of work did not stand in some soulless dole queue; he went home, to be cared for by his family. Paradoxically (although the paradox was only in our eyes) polygamy among the Moslem Hausas and Fulanis made for the strongest of family communities. I well remember Anne Sharpley, of the London *Evening Standard*, being asked on her return from Nigeria what had impressed her most during her reporting tour there. 'I think above all', she said, 'that I never heard a baby cry.'

In the expatriate community, as like as not, mother and father were separated, sons and daughters away at boarding school in the UK.

No, the learning was not all to be on the Nigerian side, socially or politically. And yet it seemed to me that we had much to give. In politics, particularly, the notion of 'Opposition' was new and could surely be valuable. I found among Nigerian politicians an innate tolerance but a complete incomprehension of the idea that political movements opposed to the established government should be allowed, even encouraged, to campaign in public against government legislation.

When I began my political commentaries on the radio, I knew that any criticism of the ruling Northern People's Congress, or praise for the rival Northern Elements Progressive Union, courted trouble. The Premier certainly had the power to take me off the air. Yet he never so much as hinted at doing so. If I said something that upset him, he would come down from Kaduna with a caravan of supporters to my Zaria office. 'I didn't like what you said last night, Michael', he'd begin, and we were launched into a long discussion about his policies and my expressed opinions of them. Not once did he use his power to prevent my talking about any policy topic on the radio, though he did his damnedest to dissuade me by rational argument.

All this time, I was not only learning about African politics and society; I was developing a love of the place that has stayed with me ever since. It is no use my attempting to define it, because so many great writers have attempted to analyse the so-called 'African Personality', or 'Negritude' as the French have it, and have largely failed. Perhaps that poet and politician Leopold Senghor has come closest to it and I think there is a fascinating clue to be found in his short poem on New York through African eyes.

Shortly before we left Nigeria, we had been to a party arranged for our farewell. (The welcome parties continued nightly for the first six months of our stay, the farewell parties for the last six.) In the morning, we were woken by the agitated knocking on the bedroom door of our houseboy, Musa. 'Come quickly', he shouted.

I emerged bleary-eyed from under the mosquito net and walked into a scene of desolation. The thieves had been in during the night and had robbed us of every possession. I mean that literally. There was not a moveable object left in the house. They had even stripped off the cushion covers.

Their method was simple. Our house had mud walls and a thatched roof. Between the top of the wall and the roof was a gap, which was an ideal design for keeping the interior cool but a godsend to thieves. They came in a group of three or four. One of them stripped naked and was covered in grease. Then 'over the top' he went, opened the windows from the inside, and passed all our belongings through to his mates. If we had disturbed them as they worked, we had no chance of catching the man on the inside because his greased body would easily have slithered out of any grasp.

As soon as we discovered the theft, we phoned the police. Oddly, although the station was only half a mile down the road, it took them a good half-hour to arrive. Oddly, too, there had been no policeman patrolling the road that night despite the fact that we paid them to do so. (It was not really odd, of course. They had been bribed by the thieves.)

Briskly, the detective sergeant mustered our household staff in the compound, questioned each one for a few minutes and then announced that he had discovered the thief. 'That's your man,' he said in the best Ealing Films tradition, 'take him away.' He looked at me proudly: 'I was trained at Scotland Yard.'

I was impressed but disbelieving that the culprit could really be our garden boy in whom I had complete trust. I wanted to know on what grounds the accusation was being made.

'It is an inside job', said the sergeant. 'He will confess. Besides, he is an Ibo.'

And that, it subsequently turned out, was the sole ground for the charge, which I would not allow and which was subsequently proved groundless. I often wondered, during the Ibo revolt and the Biafran War, whether that garden boy was still alive.

Now that slight story may seem an awful indictment of the Nigerians and their 'backward' standards, yet I do not see it that way. Corruption? We have that for sure in our own society, albeit we are rather more sophisticated about it. Wrongful arrest? We know all about that. Tribalism? We manage to kill and maim each other in Northern Ireland. No, the story for me was a comical interlude – and no one got hurt.

We went to Nigeria with two children – Mark, who was three, and Andrew who was 18 months old – and came home with three, because Eve was born out there. (The birth was not celebrated by the Africans in our house but was seen rather as a great disappointment because, of course, women were decidedly second-class citizens.)

Much of the time we were there, Andrew had been cared for by our houseboy, Musa, as though he had been his own. Back in Britain, we were worried by Andrew's decline. He lost weight. He was moody and unhappy. There was no clue to what was wrong. And then one day we showed our colour slides, as families do, to Grandma and Grandad. Among them was a picture of Musa in the garden.

Andrew came to life. He ran to the screen, pointing at it excitedly: 'Musa! Musa!' He was happy again, somehow bridging an emotional gap between two homes.

I knew how he felt.

CHAPTER THREE

Out on My Own

I was out of a job. Because Mark was approaching school age and we did not want him to be dumped in a boarding school, thousands of miles from home, we decided not to return to Africa.

That meant I was looking for work, but confident that I could pick and choose from a variety of jobs that would no doubt be offered to me. I had three months paid leave to come, so there was plenty of time to shop around – a luxury new to me. I was the world's greatest living expert on Nigerian affairs, so clearly many national newspapers would want to buy my expertise. And, with my varied journalistic experience, I could obviously pick up the editorship of any provincial newspaper I cared to choose.

That was the arrogant theory.

In practice, I bought my weekly copies of the *World's Press News*, applied for countless jobs and came up against a solid wall of disinterest. Far from being back in the mainstream, I felt almost an outcast. 'Nigeria? That's somewhere in West Africa, isn't it? You must be sadly out of touch, old boy, with affairs here at home.' That synthesised the attitude of prospective employers.

Clearing the rejection slips off my desk, I wrote a letter to the BBC, explaining that I was the greatest living etcetera, etcetera, and offering to provide a series of radio lectures on the political development of Nigeria. In retrospect it is surprising that I received even the courtesy of a reply, yet Kenneth Lamb – who was then, I believe, a radio talks producer – wrote to suggest that I might go up to Broadcasting House to see him.

When I arrived in his office, expecting to discuss whether my series should consist of six half-hour talks or perhaps ten, he greeted me with: 'Good afternoon. The tea has just arrived and I usually have mine with Jennifer Farnes-Barnes in the next office. Would you care to join us?' (I have invented her name because I have long since forgotten the real one.)

It was a 'nice' cup of tea, sugared with polite conversation. Jennifer, it turned out, was quite familiar with Nigeria and was eager to get up to date with the gossip: 'How's Sir Abubakar Tafawa Balewa these days? Such a charming man . . . Have they built the road to Maiduguri yet? . . . What do you think of the prospects of the United Middle Belt Congress at the next elections?'

Tea over, I wanted to get down to the negotiations. 'It's been a pleasure to meet you', said Kenneth Lamb. I'm sorry we can't talk further because I have an appointment. Oh, and about your suggestion for a radio talk: I'm afraid we have just commissioned William Clark to do a series on Nigeria, so it's not really feasible. But while you're in town, you might like to wander into our Overseas Service in Oxford-street. They're just starting up an African service in the vernacular and might be interested to see you. Ask for Mrs Stradling. Good afternoon.'

I was dismayed and angry. After all, he had asked me to go to London to discuss my proposals and all I'd had was a genteel cup of tea. And then, as I made my way disconsolately to Oxford street, it dawned on me that I had been thoroughly vetted. In the most pleasant possible way, my knowledge of West African affairs had been closely examined by the African expert on Kenneth's staff. And, sure enough, when I arrived at Mrs Stradling's office, the word had patently been passed down the line that I was worth some sort of trial.

My association with the BBC was about to begin. The very first talks feature to be broadcast by the newly created Hausa Section was a piece about the Grand National. Script by Michael Barratt. Translation and narration by Hausa trainees attached to the staff. There followed, I recall, a feature on tin mining in Britain and another on independence for Ghana.

I forget what the fee was – something in the region of 15 guineas (they always worked in guineas in those prosperous days) for a 15 minute script. It was hardly enough to pay the rent and feed three children, because they could not take more than one script a month, so I took a full-time job as sub-editor with the Wolverhampton *Express and Star* and later as Deputy Editor of the *Chronicle*.

Our fourth child, Paul, was born while we were in Wolverhampton. Twelve pounds, he was – the biggest to be born there since they started keeping records. It was hardly the most propitious time, financially at any rate, to 'go freelance', but in 1959 that's what I did. By then I was earning a fair amount from the Corporation by writing three scripts a week, reviews of African affairs as they were reported and discussed in the British Press. The programmes were transmitted in the Hausa, Somali and Swahili services.

I had to write them all on a Sunday because I was working on the paper during the rest of the week. And one morning, as I was sitting writing at my desk, I looked out of the window to watch other fathers pulling their children on sledges through the snow, or having snowball fights with them. That, I thought, is where I should be.

It was a snap decision, based wholly on emotion. I had no reason to expect that I could earn a decent living without a regular job, but I determined to try.

My wife Joan must have been much concerned about my prospects of paying the mortgage and feeding and clothing four children, but she did not evince the slightest anxiety. If that's what I wanted to do, that's what I must do. And the next morning I gave in my notice to the paper. It was the last time I was to have a secure job. And, as it turned out, although the decision had been made so that I might devote more hours to being a father, it was the beginning of a long period during which they rarely saw me at all.

I had spread the word around about my 'availability' but there were no assurances of any work coming my way. There were the African Service scripts, of course, yet there was no more than a three-monthly guarantee of their continuing and they did not constitute an income to live on.

The first Monday as a freelance was something of a nightmare. I sat by the phone and willed it to ring, unreasonably hoping that someone somewhere would offer me work to do. Someone, bless him, did. It was the BBC in Birmingham asking me to meet a recording car and to interview a travelling theatre director for transmission in that evening's regional news magazine. I had neither seen a recording car nor conducted a radio interview before.

I had no idea then whether the job I did was a good one or not, because nobody told me. The only clue I had was that I was asked to do another interview the next day – and the next and the next. Gradually the assignments increased and I was spending sometimes 16 hours a day charging round the country with a portable tape recorder providing two and three-minute contributions for the Midland Home Service, *Radio Newsreel*, *Today*, *The Eye-Witness* and many more. I never dared to say 'no' to any request for fear of not being asked again. Working as hard as I knew how, I was picking up enough cheques of two or three guineas each to make a living.

Nowadays, when envious staffmen comment about the money I am earning for television, I tell them: 'You, too, can earn as much. Give up your job and the security that goes with it, abandon your pension rights, and put yourself on the open market. There's a good living to be made for the few years until they tire of your face and your voice.'

Radio work led to an opportunity to contribute a brief report on a television programme in the Midlands. It came close to being my last because I learned later that one of the regional bosses there held an inquest the following day. He wanted to know who was responsible for putting 'that fellow Barratt on the screen. He has no talent and should not be used again'. I still do not know who said that, nor do I know the name of another departmental head who disagreed with his assessment and countermanded it.

The step into television was without doubt the most stimulating I ever took. Whole new dimensions of reporting were opened up. Here was the chance to do a fundamentally journalistic job with all the added tools that this visual medium had to offer. Film, videotape, studio techniques . . . I became completely absorbed in it all and set about learning its skills as fast as I could. With a little bit of luck.

The luck, if that is what it was, came by way of John Profumo. In the wake of the political scandal that shocked (or titivated) the nation for so long, *Panorama* decided to mount an item on the effects of Profumo on the grass roots of the Tory party. As part of their investigation, they required analytical reports from the South of England, the Midlands, Scotland and so on. The BBC regions involved were asked to assign their own men, and the Midlands chose me.

I approached the job with the same kind of awe that I would have felt being asked to edit *The Times*. It had seemed to me that *Panorama* was the apex of television journalism, a faraway citadel of professional excellence that I could not approach for many years. Yet here I was, less than four years after I had ventured into radio work, taking part in the programme.

Richard Dimbleby, who was to become a most valued friend and tutor, introduced the item as usual and turned to me, shivering in my timbers in that Birmingham studio, for my report. I knew that opportunity was knocking loud and clear. I did not know whether I had the ability, or the adrenalin, to open the door and grasp it.

Of all the contributions I have since made on the screen, that is the one I shall never forget. Duration: One minute.

Thenceforward, things moved fast. I was called next morning to London to see Paul Fox, then Head of Public Affairs. (I don't think he liked my disinclination to specialise, my determination to be an 'all-rounder', but I knew I had a foot in the door.) I made two films for *Panorama*, the first on the Sheffield rhino-whipping police scandal, the second on the even more notorious Rachman affair, in which I unearthed and came face to face with the inheritors of that exploiter's empire.

In 1963 I was offered a contract to join the *Panorama* team, for a year with their option on a second year. They were paying me £4,000 a year. I had arrived at Shangri-La.

And that, dear children, is how your father arrived in the big time and, unwillingly but effectively, turned his back on you for four long years.

CHAPTER FOUR
Triumphs and Disasters

MY FIRST foreign film reporting assignment for the BBC's Current (or, as it was then called, Public) Affairs Group was in Sweden; the beginning of the globtrotting years. It was for a series called *Outlook Europe* – irreverently dubbed by most of us who worked on it 'Look Out, Europe' – and it was designed to fill the eight o'clock spot on Monday nights during *Panorama's* summer break.

The producer was Jack Ashley, now an MP, who was later to become totally deaf. In his book, *Journey Into Silence*, Jack recounts how, years later, I was to be the first reporter to interview him for television after his tragic loss of hearing. 'The night it appeared on television', he writes, 'Pauline [his wife] and I were content, for we had passed a landmark together.' He was able to lip-read my questions so well that some months afterwards he agreed to a live interview in the studio – and eventually we became so bold that we conducted a two-way conversation in different studios, with me in the *Nationwide* set in London and Jack lip-reading me from a monitor in Birmingham.

Outlook Europe was, I suppose, the first in a long line of programmes leading up to our entry into the Common Market. The idea was to see how Continental countries dealt with problems that were exercising British minds at the time. Thus, from Sweden, David Dimbleby reported on the laws to combat drunken driving on the roads and I examined the modernisation of the Swedish shipbuilding industry. Jack Ashley arranged that we should all leave for Stockholm together – David, myself, director David Webster and the camera crew – which was a splendid idea as far as I was concerned because those seasoned travellers could hold my hand, but only as far as

Stockholm, because I had to leave them there to shoot their driving story while I went on alone to Gothenberg to 'recce' the shipbuilding yards.

And that is where things went sadly wrong. For a start, I found that every shipyard in the country was closed, its gates locked and its staff out of town for the annual holiday. There wasn't a soul I could see to give me any information. Anxiously, feeling that I had fallen down on my very first assignment, I phoned David Webster in Stockholm to tell him the worst. 'Can't be helped', he said. 'You'll just have to enjoy yourself. I'll be over with the crew when the yards reopen next week.'

That sounded fine, but David didn't know the acute embarrassment I was suffering. I was stoney broke. The office in London, working by its normal rules, had given me £56 advance expenses before I left. The 'daily rate' for Sweden was £7 and I was expected to be away for eight days. But they had also booked me in at the Park Avenue Hotel, not only the best in Gothenberg, but among the most expensive in the whole of Europe. My £56 was about enough for a couple of days staying there and I had taken no money of my own because I had none to take in those days. What could I do? Knowing that I could not possibly pay the hotel bill at the end of the week, I had visions of a Swedish jail and the ending in disgrace of my relationship with the BBC before it had properly begun. In the event, I did nothing, which is to say I spent hour after hour, day after day, walking the streets of Gothenberg, gazing in shop windows or sitting at the water's edge watching the jolly holiday trippers. I confined myself to one sandwich each lunch-time and the cheapest omelette on the hotel menu in the evening. I have never been so miserable in my life. When David finally arrived from Stockholm at the end of the longest week I can remember, I was half-starved and deeply depressed. I told him of my money problems.

'Ridiculous', he said. 'Never let them send you away without enough money. How much more do you need?' Because of the careful, not to say desperate, husbanding of my few kroner, I reckoned I could just pay my hotel debts with another £30 and told him so. David picked up the phone and barked down the line to our London office: 'Barratt needs another £100. Please cable it here immediately.'

The film we made then was, I suppose, competent enough, though any memory of it is obliterated. That week in Gothenberg can only be remembered for the loneliness and the hunger.

It was to be quickly followed by another trip, my first for *Panorama*, to the United States.

At the end of August, 1963, the Barratt family moved to the village of Winkfield in Berkshire, a few miles from Windsor. I was determined that we should be together from the start of my move to a London-based programme, so there was little time for house-hunting (precious little money, either) and we rented a furnished Victorian house which had been advertised as 'ideal for a family' – meaning, I think, that even the most destructive of children could not make it or its contents any more decrepit than they were. Still, we were together. For two days. On September 1, with all our own furniture still stacked higgledy-piggledy in the garage and a host of repair jobs urgently needing to be done to make the place habitable, I was packed off to America for a six-week tour with cameraman Erik Durschmeid and director Christopher Ralling. Joan and the six children would just have to make the best of it while I was away, trying to hold my own in the big league of television reporting.

I was ill-equipped for it, not because I lacked competence as a reporter (though I had so much to learn) but because I was a complete stranger in a world that was so familiar to Chris and Erik. Most of the leading figures in the American Administration were well known to them; they knew their way around the corridors of power in Washington or the boardrooms of businessmen in New York, whereas I had never even visited these cities. They would talk of 'the last time we shot President Kennedy at the White House' or something of the sort, whereas the only top people with whom I had filmed interviews up to then were the Lord Mayor of Birmingham and the manager of Wolverhampton Wanderers. The result was that I lapsed into silence for most of the trip, uneasy in their company and plagued by doubts about my ability to hold my own in the rarefied atmosphere of television reporting at their level. The old shyness returned, self-confidence drained away.

Chris naturally interpreted my manner as rudeness and quite properly berated me for it. He knew only too well something that I still had to learn – that these foreign assignments required a special effort in personal relationships. We lived in each other's pockets, day and night, for weeks on end and the success of the work we had been sent out to do depended to a great extent on each member of the team's contributing to good fellowship.

Nevertheless, despite my taciturnity, we turned in some strong films. The first took us to Birmingham, Alabama, and my first experience of racial tension and hatred, Southern-style. Two little Negro girls had died after a bomb, planted in a church, had exploded during a Sunday school lesson. I remember going to their funeral service, at which the Rev. Martin Luther King was to give the oration. Because of trade union rules, we had taken on a local sound recordist (white, of course) who was clearly ill at ease as we set up our equipment in the church among the black mourners. He referred to them as 'Niggras'. In his eyes, we were obviously Communists, traitors to the human (which is to say, white) race, breaking all his rules of normal behaviour by setting foot in a Negro church. And he did his best to sabotage our operation.

One of the problems of filming in a situation like that is the limited amount of film in the camera. Each roll lasts about ten minutes and, of course, it is very expensive, so when Mr. King went into his long address, we could not simply point the camera at him and let it run from beginning to end. We had to be selective. I therefore sat beside Erik and the sound recordist, telling them which sections of the speech I wanted. After we had less than a minute's worth 'in the can', the recordist told me that he had run out of tape. I told him to load some more, as quickly as possible. 'The rest of the tapes are in the car', he told me, 'and I had to park it two miles down the road because there was no room in front of the church' . . . Effectively, he had 'silenced' Martin Luther King and hampered our efforts to reflect the extraordinary dignity of that funeral service. The parents and relatives of the murdered black children eschewed hate (overtly, anyhow) or hysteria, seeking solace only in their God. They knew there would be no redress, no comfort from a white community of which our American 'colleague' was a typical and shameful example.

As part of the same report, I went to Montgomery to interview Governor George Wallace. This was much more to our recordist's liking and we could be sure that he would have a plentiful stock of tape available. We conducted the interview on the lawn outside the Capitol building. Most of the gubernatorial staff came out like a band of cheer leaders to applaud his oratory and to laugh at his racist jokes. Wallace's attitude sickened me. He produced all the old rubbish about the brains of Negroes (he called them 'Niggras', too) being smaller than ours. He even went into the 'would-you-let-your-daughter-marry-a-black' routine. The more I questioned, the louder he shouted, egged on by his cohorts. He turned an interview into an argument and tried to bully me into submission. Later, when the completed film was transmitted back home, that interview led Maurice Wiggin in the *Sunday Times* to describe me as a 'terrier' and to welcome me to the *Panorama* team as a reporter 'in the true Panorama mould'.

On that first filming tour for the programme I also reported from Houston on the race to the Moon, from Washington on the Joe Valachi hearings which exposed many of the activities of the Mafia, or Cosa Nostra, in the States, and from Montreal on the terrorist campaign for French separatism – a story which landed me in jail, as I shall describe later. Professionally, it was a successful trip for me and did wonders for my self-confidence. I needed that. But there were disasters ahead.

The first came one Monday evening when Editor David Wheeler decided that we should have a live studio item on a proposed substantial increase in MP's pay. It was an issue that had naturally caused a good deal of controversy around the country and we looked like having a lively 'punch-up', as it's known in the trade, to enliven our output that evening. Tom Driberg and the late Charles Curran were booked as the two combatants, with me in the middle. It didn't appear to require much homework on my part: I was assured that the two men were bitterly opposed on the issue and that my chief problem would be to discipline the discussion and perhaps keep them from coming to blows.

In the event, the 'row' turned out to be a mild assertion by both men that they supported the proposals. There seemed to be no area of disagreement or argument between them whatsoever. To my squirming embarrassment, the topic seemed to be exhausted after only a minute or so of discussion. Frantically I cast around for some angle on the subject that would bring life into the dying proceedings, but I failed abysmally. It must still rank as one of the lamest items ever mounted on television. Whether Curran and Driberg had privately agreed beforehand to take a mutual line, or whether the production assistant concerned had simply booked the wrong men, I shall never know. And I shall never forget the sequel.

At that time, Grace Wyndham Goldie, now retired, ruled the television talks empire with an imperious if sometimes wayward brilliance. Every Monday evening, she would descend on the *Panorama* hospitality room after the programme and pronounce judgement, brooking no argument. The old hands had learned to suffer her slings and arrows; I was petrified by her, not only because of her awesome reputation in the medium as the architect – perhaps genius is a better word – of programmes like *Tonight* and *Panorama* itself, but also because as Head of Department she held my future career in her hands. I would be 'one of Grace's boys' or I would be out on my neck. There were a couple of months to go before the decision was to be made whether or not my contract would be renewed . . .

'Tell me, Michael', said Grace that night, 'what are you going to do when your contract expires? Take up farming?'

It was the end of the world. She took me apart, piece by piece, and threw any self-confidence I had been developing to the winds as she enumerated the ways I had failed that night. Worse, she did this in the presence of Charles Curran who, beside being an MP, was a columnist for the London *Evening News*. I shuddered to think of the story he might write the next day of how a television reporter, rapidly becoming a nationally known figure, bit the dust. (I should have known better: there is an unspoken rule that conversations in those hospitality rooms are never revealed outside.)

Grace's demolition job was, I now know, part of the essential training process and was certainly done without malice. (She has, indeed, recently written in *The Listener* of 'the personal qualities of Michael Barratt, who is able to put shrewd and penetrating questions without ever losing his earthbound good humour'. I thank her for that, as I do for her criticisms in the early days.)

I had much, much more to learn and my second real disaster was also one of my best-remembered lessons. It arose from a special programme we mounted on the Buchanan Report, instigated by the then Minister of Transport, Ernest Marples. I had to introduce the programme and interview the Minister. It went out quite late in the evening and when Ernest arrived at the studios, it was clear that he had come from a very good meal. Not to put too fine a point on it, let's say that the wine must have flowed freely. One of his worried aides took me to one side. 'You will appreciate', he said, 'that the Minister is very tired. I hope you will understand and not give him too rough a ride.'

We went into the studio and Ernest demanded a drink. The floor manager said she was very sorry, we had nothing but water. This greatly displeased him and for a moment I thought he was going to walk out. I determined to lob some exceedingly soft questions to him, hoping that his 'tiredness' would not be too evident to viewers.

'Minister,' I began, 'this report calls for planning on a national basis. I'm surprised that you endorse its findings, because as a Conservative you are in principle opposed to this kind of planning.'

Suddenly Ernest Marples was no longer tired. He was as sharp as a pin. He rounded on me: 'When have I said that?'

'Well . . .' I floundered.

'Come on, Mr. Barratt, I want chapter and verse. Quote me the time and place that I have opposed planning.' I couldn't.

'Please withdraw that question, then.' I withdrew in some confusion and tried another tack. But he hadn't finished with me. Responding to my next question, he said:

'You don't appear to understand the nature of our problem. Do you know the number of cars per mile of highway in Great Britain compared to the figure in the United States?' I hoped that was a rhetorical question. No such luck. 'Do you?' he pressed. I confessed that I had no idea, but that was not enough. 'Have a guess', he insisted.

To say that Ernest Marples took me to the cleaners that night would be a hopeless understatement. In his hands I was more like a wet sponge in a mangle. And next morning, as I deserved, there was a stern reprimand from my superiors at the BBC, this time in the person of Paul Fox who quite properly commented on my lazy lack of preparedness for that interview. I had a long way to go before I could lay any claim to being a skilled reporter or interviewer.

CHAPTER FIVE
A Great Man

OF ALL the influences that have made up the me that is me now, few have been as profound as that of Albert Schweitzer.

To say that is not to imply that I became, when I met him, an unquestioning disciple. There were aspects of the man and of his philosophy as he practised it that I found distasteful or disturbing. Yet if I were now asked to state my own religion or philosophy, I would describe it in his phrase: Reverence for Life.

I have been asked a thousand times to distil my reactions to my unique visit to Lambarene as an answer to the question: 'What sort of man was Schweitzer?'

In shorthand, I can answer: he was a great man. That is not to say he was a saintly man, or a progressive, or even a kindly man. Indeed, it is not to say anything at all.

People, even if their name is Albert Schweitzer, cannot be seen in isolation. Nor can one's assessment of them be wholly objective; it must be related, for instance, to the circumstances of meeting, even to the logistics of effecting a meeting.

I met Schweitzer in the jungle, not on the concert platform. I was a television reporter, not a patient. We spoke different languages. The details are important.

On a January evening in 1965, Richard Dimbleby turned to Camera One and said: 'As far removed as he could be from the hurly-burly of politics and, indeed, from the whole Western world, a man whose name is known everywhere is celebrating his ninetieth birthday – Albert Schweitzer, theologian, missionary, organist, surgeon.

'This is a man whom some people have turned almost into a saint in his own lifetime, brilliant at everything he's touched and yet devoted to the care of suffering people.

'But in recent years some have doubted the legend of Schweitzer and the value of the pioneer leper hospital which he founded 50 years ago deep in the African Republic of Gabon at Lambarene. To see for himself, Michael Barratt went to visit Albert Schweitzer at Lambarene.'

Before I set off on that memorable visit, I had done my homework. I had read Schweitzer's writings and had become fascinated (if not wholly convinced) by his philosophy of Reverence for Life. And I had come up against so many paradoxes.

There was his pessimism about the decay of our civilisation which had persisted since his undergraduate days when he sombrely believed that the fire of mankind's ideals 'was already burning low without anyone noticing it, or troubling about it . . . My own impression was that in our mental and spiritual life we were not only below the level of past generations, but were in many respects only living on their achievements – and that not a little of this heritage was beginning to melt away in our hands'.

On the other side of the coin was the essential optimism of his belief that everyone – human beings, animals, even the flowers of the field – shared what he called the will-to-live. The nature of this will-to-live, he said, 'carries within it the impulse to realise itself in the highest possible perfection'.

Again: 'If I save an insect from a puddle, life has devoted itself to life and the division of life against itself ended. Whenever my life devotes itself in any way to life, my finite will-to-live experiences union with the infinite will which in all life is one.'

With these and so many more pieces of the complex Schweitzer jigsaw tumbling around in my head, I set off for Lambarene with producer Dick Francis and cameraman Eric Durschmeid. I am sure none of us had the faintest idea what kind of film would emerge from our trip and I suspect we all had private doubts about our ability to make any meaningful assessment of the man in the space of a few thousand feet of film.

The journey took us from London to Kano, Lagos, Daccar and Libreville. There, we loaded our gear on an ancient Dakota which could be described as a 'passenger plane' only in the sense that it had some narrow and extremely hard seats screwed into its bare aluminium floor.

It was replete with insects. Its air conditioning in the humid equatorial heat consisted of tiny fans fixed to the luggage rack above our heads.

Our fellow passengers were Africans, most of whom were violently sick on take-off and continued to be throughout the rest of the journey. Their vomit (forgive the crudities, but it *was* a crude flight) flowed sluggishly down the aisle towards the tail end of the plane. And then we ran into a tropical thunderstorm. The little plane was thrown around in the sky as the lightning flashed all around us. I was not, at the time, thinking of Albert Schweitzer yet I did, in some terror, learn a thing or two about the 'will to live'.

At last, coming in to land on the strip at Lambarene township, we were met by a doctor and a nurse from Schweitzer's hospital. We had also been joined in the last stages of our journey by Pastor Niemuller from Germany, who had been deeply influenced as a young man by Schweitzer the theologian and later by Schweitzer the philosopher. Now he was coming to see Schweitzer the doctor at work and to share in the celebration of his birthday.

Together we carried our equipment down to the muddy edge of the Ogowe river. Waiting to carry us to the extraordinary world Albert Schweitzer had hacked out of the jungle more than half a century earlier were two pirogues – unstable vessels like canoes which are carved from the trunk of a tree. The men who paddled them were lepers.

It seemed an immediate confirmation of the charges made by Schweitzer's detractors – charges that he deliberately fought 'progress' and that by turning his back on 'civilisation' he even hampered his own work. I knew that, more than once, the Doctor had been offered the gift of a powered boat to take people and supplies up the Ogowe, and that he had turned down every offer. Yet it was too easy to misconstrue his attitude as I discovered several days later when Schweitzer talked to me about those pirogues. 'Unlike motor boats,' he said, 'craft paddled by men do not break down. They do not require expert and expensive maintenance. And I ask you: why should we be in such a hurry?'

It is nevertheless a tortuous journey by pirogue to Lambarene. I blanched at the information that the river abounded with hippos and crocodiles, but the doctor who had been sent to guide us to the hospital thought he was comforting me with the assurance that they were no real danger. Much more perilous were the swarms of lethal electric fish unseen in the muddy waters. 'We were unfortunate enough to lose one of our staff last week when he fell overboard into a shoal of them.'

And then another sharp reminder that we had entered a different world: when Eric assembled his camera, the entire expedition nearly came to an abrupt end. The African paddlers went berserk. The pirogues nearly overturned as the men flung their arms about and screamed at Eric to put his camera away. They still believed that a camera, with its power to capture a man's image, also had the power to capture his soul.

Back on a stable course again, we rounded the last bend to see ahead the clearing in the jungle that was Schweitzer's hospital community. Our arrival was a well staged production which would have done any modern film director credit. As we approached the shore, a call from one of the boatmen was the cue for Herr Doktor to walk through the trees and down to the water's edge to greet us. He might have been rehearsing the timing for days. And then I shook hands with this slightly stooping but teak-tough man, about to enter his ninety-first year, in his home where few half his age could survive for very long.

Schweitzer had once said – in the days of deep pessimism about the degeneracy of civilisation – that 'it was becoming more and more difficult to be a personality'. I was quickly to learn that here was a personality who totally dominated the community he had created. He strode through his world, impervious to criticism from outside and deaf to it from people around him. He was the lawmaker and his laws, however seemingly insignificant some of them were, became inviolable.

As soon as the formal greetings were over, we were led to the wooden hut where we were to spend the next few days at Lambarene – and we were each presented with a typed list of rules which all visitors, as well as staff, must obey. We read that under no circumstances were we to go outside without wearing a pith helmet. It was absolutely forbidden to kill any of the insects which abounded in the huts. (An aerosol spray for killing mosquitoes which I had brought with me began to take on the form of a hydrogen bomb.)

A first walk round Schweitzer's village seemed to confirm the criticisms that it was appallingly insanitary for medical work. For the five hundred Africans there at the time, there was no lavatory of any kind, just the jungle. Goats and hens, dogs and cats, roamed around at will. People who were perfectly fit lived with those who were desperately ill. African patients who came for treatment simply brought their family and their animals along with them. Schweitzer liked it that way – and it is not difficult to find eminent specialists around today who will argue in favour of his kind of psycho-therapy as a 'step forward' in hospital treatment. Schweitzer had been practising it for half a century.

Any member of his staff who disliked the insanitary nature of the place had only one method of protest – and that was to leave. Many of them had done. Others, a select few who were very close to him, gave him their lives with unquestioning loyalty. Ali Silver, from Holland, was one of those whom we came to call his 'angels'. She had then been at Lambarene for 17 years and she was convinced that the community had been tailored to the African way of life. It would not have occurred to her, I suspect, to ask whether this 'African way of life' might not be ideal. And there is no doubt that Schweitzer's Lambarene was what so many Africans themselves wanted. Some of the older patients, cured of an illness, would ask to be allowed to stay there for the rest of their days.

The Doctor seemed to treat most Africans with some degree of disdain. As we walked round with him, shooting film, he displayed a charming bedside manner and he would often stop to pat the head of a child or shake the hand of an old man. But we were beginning to learn that Albert Schweitzer was no mean actor and one of the staff told me that those gestures were seen only when the cameras were turning or a visitor was staying there.

His staff was exclusively white. He could, and did, argue that there were no qualified Africans available to take over important duties, but on the other hand I could find no evidence that there was any significant effort to train them.

Many of the hospital's facilities were crude by any Western standards, but again Schweitzer's absolute faith in his own methods was reflected in the Africans' faith in him. Some of them walked three hundred miles through the jungle to find him rather than enter the government's impeccably sanitary and well-equipped but soulless hospitals in Lambarene township downriver or in Libreville.

Schweitzer's own health and strength were partly due to his own personal discipline. He never smoked. He never ate meat. He never drank more than a small glass of beer. He rarely even sat down, preferring to walk around the village or work on some building project. Yet all this was surely insufficient explanation of his remarkable physical resilience. Surely, too, there was an element of spiritual drive behind it.

The only time I saw him taking to the jeep was when we visited the leper village, which was rebuilt with his Nobel Prize money and which stood apart from the main community. There were 250 lepers there at the time, under Schweitzer's general direction (of course) but in the immediate care of a Japanese helper who, like so many others, had visited Lambarene to learn something of the Doctor's philosophy. He stayed, because he had become another of the 'disciples' and at the same time he had developed a special affection for the lepers.

Much has been written, some of it cynically, about the attraction Schweitzer seemed to have for wealthy women. When I was there, another visitor was the wealthy New Yorker Mrs Myer, formerly Otto Preminger's wife. She used to go to Lambarene every year about the time of the Doctor's birthday to take clothing and presents for the lepers; she encouraged them to call her 'Mother Marian'. Like the others, Mrs Myer never thought of questioning Schweitzer's methods of running the community.

She told me, 'I know the hospital has no water, no light, no electricity' (this was not strictly true, as we shall see), 'but this is still a lighthouse to all other hospitals. Perhaps this is the only place that feeds, houses, clothes and medicates all its patients – and medicates with that very important medicine, human kindness. Reverence for Life, his philosophy, has become also my philosophy. And, you know, when a sage gets to be ninety years old, you don't question him any more.'

And yet, of course, there *were* questions to be asked about his philosophy, questions with which the old man was still wrestling in his own brilliant mind. There was no doubt that his own 'reverence for life' was all-embracing. Sometimes we learned that the hard way – like the morning when Eric was filming a sequence with Ali Silver and stepped on a nest of ants which swarmed over him and nipped him sorely. He began to brush them off but the nurse, horrified, stopped him and began to pick the ants off his body gently 'so as not to hurt the poor creatures'.

We were reminded again and again of the cardinal rule that to strike off in thoughtless pastime the head of a single flower was a wrong against life. Yet it was said to be consistent with this ethic that plant life might be cultivated and then cut down in order to feed the village. As the questions grew in my mind, so the answers seemed to slip further out of my grasp.

Schweitzer's relationship with the jungle that surrounded him contained the same seeming paradoxes. He looked upon it as a world in which every leaf, every insect was a precious life with its own will-to-live. To enter the jungle outside the community was forbidden. And yet he spent much of his energy hacking away at that same jungle, preventing its encroachment on the village.

This and the rest of the daily work, he alone organised like some military commander. Twice a day, the able-bodied Africans mustered (in ragged ranks but nonetheless 'to attention') below his office to be given their orders. The women were detailed jobs like washing clothes, always under white supervision. Schweitzer himself would march off with a party of men to oversee building operations, which had become his own main activity since virtually retiring from medical work.

The reward for the workers was food. Men and women of a dozen tribes queued up each day for the distribution of manioc, a plant which is like the texture of bread, packed in leaves. They would take it away to feed their relatives, the patients often squatting by wood fires to cook their meals. For another element of the Schweitzer 'psycho-therapy' was home cooking.

Despite what Mrs Myer had told me, there was an electricity generating plant in the village, used mainly to light and power the operating rooms. Yet – another of those endless paradoxes – he refused to use electricity for lighting rooms in the hospital and in the evening at supper time, doctors and nurses and visitors like ourselves were required to pick our way through the trees with storm lanterns to the hut that was the staff dining room.

It was this room, which might better be described as a sanctuary, which perhaps left the deepest impression on me. Supper time was the culmination of Schweitzer's day and the room in which we ate had become so precious to him that it was the one place where he refused to let our cameras or sound equipment intrude.

Each night, like the children of some Victorian family, we filed in to stand behind our chairs until the master arrived with one of his 'angels'. Nobody sat down until he had done so. Nobody spoke to him until they were spoken to.

The meals were varied and good. Although Schweitzer kept to his own special diet, the rest of us fed well on dishes like roast crocodile and fresh fruit. It was, however, absolutely forbidden to leave any food on our plates uneaten. I assumed that the reasoning behind this rule was the belief that, though life had to be taken to preserve life, nevertheless it was evil to take more life than was absolutely necessary.

There was, however, one way of circumventing the rule. The staff had learned to keep side plates on which they placed any uneaten food. This, they said, was to feed their pets – which seemed to comply with the master's orders.

After eating, the old man would stand up and walk over to an old, ill-tuned upright piano and lead us all in hymn-singing. (For the musical genius who was probably the world's greatest authority on Bach, an out-of-tune piano must have given pain. But no piano could stand up to that climate.) After the hymns, Schweitzer would take his place at the table again and read a passage from the Bible in German and then the same passage again in his guttural French.

The last stage of the nightly ritual varied. The Doctor might be in a mood for small-talk or decide to deliver a sermon on the text he had just read. Here I remembered the story of his decision to go to Africa as doctor rather than missionary 'so that I might be able to work without having to talk'. Scratch the doctor and there, unmistakeably, was the zealous missionary beneath the skin.

On the nights that he wanted to indulge in small-talk, his audience was a captive one. Nobody ever interrupted him, though they were careful to laugh at the right places. Some of them took notes of what he said, however inconsequential it might seem. But nobody ever argued with the autocrat of the supper table.

Again the charge could be made: This way of life was all very well for Schweitzer himself but unnatural for everybody else. I put this point to Pastor Niemuller, who as a life-long friend was closer to the Doctor than a mere television reporter would ever hope to be.

He said, 'I think this way of life is very near to the feelings of the people with whom Dr Schweitzer has to work here and whom he has to serve. He has to live this way and the people respond to it. I could not imagine this village continuing to exist except with the kind of autocratic superiority which he has acquired in a long life of service.'

It was not until the end of our visit to Lambarene that I talked at any length to Schweitzer himself. After soaking in as much as I could of his 'reverence for life' as he had put it into practice, I wanted to know above all in what ways – and after so many years – his passionate beliefs had been tempered or even changed by harsh experience.

Yet he told me that if he were to rewrite then (and he was still writing) the volumes he had written so long before about the philosophy of civilisation, he would make no significant changes. He still believed, for instance, that 'while animals have to endure intolerable treatment from heartless men, we will share the guilt'.

Most questions were brushed aside. At ninety, he was still

a man in a hurry, convinced that he still had many years to live yet somehow, too, obsessed by the idea that he had so little time left to make his philosophy bear fruit in the world.

As we talked in Lambarene, back in London the pundits were earnestly and angrily debating the 'wind of change' in Africa. Issues like 'one man, one vote' and independence for the remaining colonies were exercising the minds of our leading politicians and intellectuals.

I had a fanciful vision of Albert Schweitzer striding into one of our studios, exclaiming, 'Ethics are responsibility without limit towards all that lives' – and striding out again.

Perhaps he would have been saying more than the rest of us have been trying to say for years.

CHAPTER SIX
The Family Way

PUBLIC EXPOSURE makes personal privacy so vulnerable as to be almost an impossibility.

Paradoxically, the incessant search in the public prints for 'the real man' behind a so-called popular personality leads only to unreality. To hold on to one's own identity becomes increasingly difficult.

I remember one night in the *Nationwide* studio when we were discussing a new book about bringing up young children. To ask the questions of the author, we brought in my colleague from Bristol, Amanda Theunissen, because she had recently given birth to a baby daughter – the first to be born to any of our reporters since the programme's inception.

Amanda had the baby on her lap in the studio and I welcomed her as 'our first Nationwide baby'.

Some weeks later, Amanda was on holiday in Devon, pushing the pram.

An old lady stopped her. 'Don't tell me, I know – you're Amanda Theunissen', she said, and peered into the pram. 'Oh, what a lovely baby. Mr Barratt must be so pleased.'

'But it's not his baby', protested Amanda.

'Yes it is, he told us so the other night', corrected the lady.

Amanda insisted that she was happily married and so was I, that indeed I had six children of my own and that this baby was nothing to do with me.

The old lady gave her what's commonly called an old-fashioned look and walked on, saying, 'You television people. You're all the same'.

This notion that we lead unorthodox lives, with unusual moral codes of our own, is hard to dispel. Few people seem able to believe that we may be just as happily, or unhappily, married as anyone else – or that we may experience the same traumas in the course of bringing up our children.

Yet I must be careful not to protest too much. There *are* differences; there are pressures which make 'normal' family life and social behaviour difficult, and I often wonder whether my own progress towards some prominence, or notoriety, in television has meant too high a price being paid by my wife and family. How much damage have I inflicted on them? Perhaps it is as well for my own peace of mind that it can never be accurately measured, but I cannot ignore it.

For a start, there were the days of my being an absentee father, months on end when my only contact with the family was on the backs of postcards despatched from the ends of the earth. I think the worst part about all that travelling was the homecoming – often exhausted, irritable, wanting only to get some sleep in a comfortable bed, sometimes even unaware of what day it was as my body and mind struggled to cope with a time scale that was still half a world away. I might have been away five or six weeks – how could the young children expect me to be other than 'glad to be home', eager to relax and play games with them and chatter about my experiences? How could they rationalise my tense, ill-tempered don't-bother-me re-actions to their exhuberant 'welcome home'.

In time, they learned to cope with this, to 'understand'. Neither they nor I realised then the damage that was so in-sidiously being done. Only slowly did the evidence come to the surface.

I remember on one trip receiving a letter from Joan in which she told me that Paul, who was then I suppose about eight years old, had suddenly one morning refused to go to school. He had stood with his back against the wall by the front door, fists clenched, immovable. Joan let him be – but the next day he had acted in the same way, unresponsive to reasoning, completely resistant to coaxing.

When I came home, there was still no explanation why Paul did not want to go to school, so Paul and I had a 'little chat' in the place always reserved for such things, the bathroom. (It was my habit in those days to lie in the bath and have a sing-song with the children.) After we had chatted about this and that, the question of school came up and, haltingly, Paul told me that the trouble was the school dinners which he couldn't bear to eat. So we agreed that, for a little while at least, he would come home for lunch. The next morning, perfectly content, he went to school.

Now you may think that is a pointless little story. But there is a telling sequel. A week or so later, I left on another film reporting assignment. And the next morning, Paul refused to go to school. His was no conscious protest about my being away; I am convinced that he could not explain his action even to himself. It was a danger signal to which I took too long to respond.

There were others. Like the time that Eve was preparing for her 11-plus exam – an exam which her two elder brothers had passed with ease, but which school reports suggested she might fail. I went to talk to her teacher in the little village school, to ask whether extra professional tuition at home in the evenings might help.

'It would make no difference whatsoever', said the teacher. 'Whether Eve passes or not will depend entirely on whether you are at home or away . . . Every morning as I walk into class, one glance at her will tell me. If you are away, I know that she will get all her sums wrong and the standard of all her work will be low. When you are home, she will display an intelligence and enthusiasm far above average. There are days, special days, when I see a light in her eyes and I know she will be coming to me at break to say, "Daddy's coming home today".'

What was I destroying in pursuit of a career?

As it turned out, Eve sat her exam one day when I was abroad. She failed. The headmaster advised the Authority that her paper had not been a true reflection of her ability and secured for her a second chance. This time I was at home. This time she passed.

In retrospect, such experience may seem to have been blatant evidence that my frequent absence, even alienation, from the family was having serious repercussions. But only in retrospect. At the time, almost blinded by my immersion in the job (which of course I thoroughly enjoyed) the danger signals were often unseen and for several years unheeded.

However there were, and are, other ill effects of perpetual public exposure to which I have found no real antidote. I could seek, and eventually secure, a studio-based role in television which put an end to my absences while still bringing home the bread – but what could I do to arrest the corrosion of personal identity among the rest of the family? They were all labelled. 'Michael Barratt's wife. Michael Barratt's son. Michael Barratt's daughter.'

Once, at school, our son Andrew brought his own protest to a head by giving notice to pupils and teachers: 'From now on, I wish to be known as Horace Smith.' Paradoxically, everyone laughed because that was 'just like Andrew', a boy with all the individualism you could wish for. Yet I knew how he felt and wished, with frustrating impotence, that I could help.

Similarly our eldest son, Mark, insisted for two long years that he had no idea what career he intended to pursue, although I was certain (but did not tell him so) that he shared my passion – not too strong a word – for journalism. The deterrent to his joining a newspaper was simply his fear that, in the same world as my own, any progress he made might be put down to 'father's influence'. Ultimately, thank God, the passion was too strong for the fear and he is now proving his real, and again highly individualistic, worth as a local newspaper reporter.

Because of these peculiar stresses, I treasure what we can retain of the ordinariness of home life – the ordinary stresses, if you like – such as the Monday morning ritual . . .

It's known as the school run. It ought to be called the drive to dementia.

Each morning around 8.15 a group of cars converge on the centre of our village, disgorge some of their youthful passengers, and then drive on with the remainder of their load. There is a tendency for the drivers' hair to be standing on end, for a haggard look on their faces and sometimes even a glint of violence in their eyes. We're all the same – loving fathers taking our dear children to the bus stop or to school. I have been doing some research in the area and find that my own experience is shared by all my fellow father figures, except that I lay claim to the worst ordeals through sheer force of numbers.

The school run really begins at the breakfast table.

'Where's the hair brush?'

'How do I know? Andrew had it last.'

'Don't be stupid. We go through this every morning and we always find it in Jane's room.'

'That's a lie. Anyway, it's *my* brush. You're just too lazy to look for your own. I bet Eve's using it.'

'You must be joking. You don't think I'd use the boys' brush on *my* hair, do you?'

In the mounting crescendo of charge and counter-charge, I raise my voice just enough to be heard (which mean I fill my lungs and bellow), 'We leave in five minutes. Anyone who's not ready will be left behind.'

Panic stations. Where's my case/homework/library book/shoe polish/shoes/pen/handbag/trousers/etcetera?

Trying to ignore the hullabaloo, but wondering whether ear muffs might prevent damage to my hearing, I go to the car and start up. The lemmings come tumbling out.

'I'm in the front.'

'No you're not. I always sit in the front.'

'It's my turn to sit by the door.'

'Stop arguing Paul, and get in.'

'How can I be expected to get in if Rachel won't budge up?'

'Do you mind? I'm standing in the rain, you know, and would be most grateful if my brothers and sisters would let me into the car.'

We move off and the din subsides. A happy family, silently nursing their grievances against each other. With a bit of luck, there won't be another word spoken until we arrive at the bus stop.

Then we get into the realms of high finance.

Every Monday, it's 60p for Andrew's dinner money plus 12p for the bus to school; Eve's daily 50p for lunch and bus fare to the hairdressing academy; 60p plus 20p for Paul; 9p for Jane to her school; 60p for Rachel's dinner money at the village primary school.

Making sure I have the exact coinage for all that lot means robbing our friendly newsagent of all his small change. But that's only a beginning:

'I need some money for a new pen/writing pad/school outing/ collection for black babies/geometry set/etcetra.'

The cacophony at last become unbearable. My normal composure cracks under the strain.

'Get out!' I scream, only just forbearing to add, 'and don't come back.'

Arriving home in a state of shock, I decide that something must be done about our family mornings. I'm still searching for a way to turn that drive to dementia into something more like a happy family outing.

My fellow fathers would welcome suggestions, too. But don't suggest drowning the children. We've already thought of that.

CHAPTER SEVEN

Ordeal by Election

THE UNIVERSITY of Aberdeen is one of our most ancient places of advanced learning. It likes to boast that when there were only two universities in the whole of England, Oxford and Cambridge, there were two in Aberdeen – King's which was established in 1494 to teach 'theology and canon and civil law and medicine and the liberal arts', and Marischal, which was a product of the Reformation and was endowed with buildings, lands and rents taken from the Roman Church. The two were made one in 1860. Today, the university has nearly six thousand students – growing fast towards the 10,000 mark – and an academic reputation to match its longevity. It also has a Lord Rector. Me.

Now that seems extraordinary enough to warrant some explanation.

One evening in October 1972 I came out of the studio to take a phone call from Aberdeen. 'We are about to hold elections for the office of Rector', said the voice at the other end, 'and I represent a group of students who want to nominate you. Will you consider standing?' I knew too little about the office, the work it would entail and the demands it might make, to give them an instant reply, so I arranged to fly to the Granite City and talk it over.

At that time, Jo Grimond was coming to the end of his three-year term as Rector. He followed a distinguished line which included such names as Winston Churchill, Stafford Cripps, Walter Elliott, John Buchan. Even as a prospective candidate, I felt awesomely undistinguished, but it was soon impressed on me that the nature of the office was changing with the times. The popular student cry was for 'a working Rector'. Jo

Grimond had certainly been that, though because he was typically unostentatious about the way he fulfilled his role, he came in for some criticism from the more militant factions whose cruel jibes I was soon to suffer.

I arrived in Aberdeen to find that there were already four candidates in the field. The 'student Rector' tide seemed to be running strong. John Aitken seemed the least serious contender and I do not think he ever rated his own chances very highly, though he was clearly liked by those who knew him well and his distinct lack of pomposity was an attractive asset. A much more serious contender was Alan Reay, enthusiastically backed by Left-wingers in particular, with a hard-working group of fellow students working on his campaign and a constant stream of 'newsletters' calling for more student participation in, or even control of, university administration. The front-runner appeared to be the Rev. Tom Tait, Aberdeen graduate, former president of the Students' Representative Council and now a Church of Scotland Minister in Blairgowrie. He had been given the official backing of the SRC, which looked like a trump card at the time. He could claim to understand the needs of students and the machinery of university government like the Court, the Senatus Academicus and the multifarious committees.

The fourth candidate was Russell Hunter, best known then – in the South, at least – as the actor who played Lonely in the Callan television series, and much respected in his own country over the years for his social involvement. He, too, had a strong campaign committee behind him.

The Rector's role was, and is, ill-defined. The office carries the right to preside over the Court, which is the university's ultimate governing body, and to a casting vote on it. This right had rarely been exercised in the past, although Jo Grimond had seldom missed a meeting. Clearly, as the Rector is elected by students only, he is their direct representative, but how and where he represents them remains far from clear. At the time I was being pressed to make a bid for the job – unpaid, largely unsung and often uncomfortable – there was a good deal of unrest in the student world. The NUS campaign for higher grants was getting under way; there were growing calls for a rent strike; Stirling was going through its own particular trauma because a handful of students had been rude to the Queen. While Aberdeen had less overt discontent than most other universities in the land, it was obvious that the Rector's lot over the following three years was not going to be an entirely happy one. So why did I agree to stand? That's a question I was asked over and over again during the campaign. I am still not sure that I know the answer myself.

To be asked, of course, was a great honour, or so it seems to me. More important, perhaps, was that the people who did the asking felt that I had something to contribute to the life of the university. If they were right, would I have been failing in my obligations by turning them down? The question supposes that I have obligations of this kind. I believe this to be so. It is often said that the so-called household names of television have an influence over public opinion out of all proportion to their talents or their worth and that this influence is improper, immoral and downright dangerous. But if this influence is as powerful as many argue, what an opportunity it gives us to make a beneficial contribution to society at all levels! More than an opportunity – an obligation. Thus, at the simplest level, if I can sell my autograph at fivepence a time to raise funds for, say, mentally handicapped children, then I must do so. The fact that I may be a brainless nincompoop is, in that context, irrelevant.

That factor, then, was much in my mind when I accepted nomination for the Rectorial. There were others – like a certain nostalgia for a city I had enjoyed in the earliest days as a reporter, and a feeling that this was somehow repaying a debt to my father. Whatever the deepest, maybe unconscious motive, I said 'yes' to my sponsors and plunged into a campaign that was variously stimulating, embarrassing, painful, exciting and completely exhausting.

Immediately I was drawn into the sort of campaign activities which I had so often derided in other candidates for other elections. True, there were no babies to be kissed, but there were hands by the hundred to be shaken, a smile to be perpetually worn – and promises, promises to be made so often that they seemed to fray at the edges. It was my first depressing

Installation as Rector of the University of Aberdeen was an awesome occasion. It was also a peculiar mixture of academic dignity and student jollity . . .

After the ceremony of capping and the speech, I was carried by
my supporters to the traditional celebration – in the pub
across the road.

Pictures by Scottish Daily Express

lesson of electioneering that declarations of intent, honestly made (and, since then, honestly fulfilled) became devalued in my own ears as a consequence of constant reiteration.

For my opponents, I was in many respects an easy target. As an Englishman, living in faraway Berkshire and with well-known professional commitments, I was the candidate who, if elected, would be an 'absentee Rector', rarely to be seen in the university and clearly unable to attend even the monthly Court meetings. The local paper tackled me on this point and I countered with the comment that it was arrant nonsense. 'Aberdeen is on my doorstep', I argued with conviction. 'It takes me just two hours to get here – not much longer than many people spend getting to work each day.' The day that story appeared in the *Aberdeen Evening Express*, I was booked on the 3.30 flight back. Home for tea was the idea. In fact, because of fog and ice at Dyce airport, I found myself on a draughty bus to Inverness – a three-hour journey – and eventually landed at Heathrow at midnight.

If the travelling became more than I had bargained for, the fierceness of the campaign battle certainly was. I was mercilessly lampooned in the columns of *Gaudie*, the student newspaper. I was taunted as 'Jelly Baby Barratt', whose election would be 'a disaster'. My opponents' literature concentrated more and more as the weeks went by on what became a sort of joint 'stop Barratt' campaign. I felt isolated and vulnerable. Yet things began to move my way.

My first real trial by fire was a mass meeting at which all the candidates were given five minutes to outline their policies, after which the hundreds of students present could ask questions. It was bedlam, with paper darts and other missiles flying all over the place and continuous roars of derision from the different groups of supporters. This was a very different kettle of fish from talking with impunity to a lifeless camera. I decided on a twin tactical approach – to wait for the noise to subside before speaking, after I had got to my feet, and to concentrate on positive and constructive ideas rather than sniping at my opponents as they were doing at me. We maintained that approach throughout the campaign and it paid handsome dividends.

Gauging the mood and the needs of the students was difficult, mainly because the voice of the militant 'student power' was so loud that it came close to drowning the others. There were demands for majority student representation on the Court, for student vetting of the academic staff, for mass marches on Stirling, rent strikes and goodness knows what else. All rousing stuff, I suppose, but hardly representative of the majority opinion. (Those who did not go along with the militants, of course, were branded as 'apathetic'.)

For my part, I promised to support a reasoned, as opposed to a self-wounding, campaign for higher grants. I promised to appoint a student Assessor on the Court. I promised to be 'on call' at all times for students who needed my help, circulating my home address and telephone number. I promised to tackle such problems as the unavailability of textbooks at the only educational bookshop in the city. I promised to work for the strengthening of good relations between staff and students, a precious asset at Aberdeen. I promised to improve communications within the university so that there would be a better understanding of the Court's functioning and suchlike.

Towards the end of the campaign, *Gaudie* held a poll which put me in high spirits but greatly alarmed the young law student who had nominated me. It made me a clear favourite to win the election. The danger, of course, was that my potential voters might be persuaded that there was little need to go to the poll.

On the eve of voting, after an uproarious and, as far as I could judge, quite pointless 'hecklers' meeting', my supporters worked through the night plastering the place with my posters. They finished at about 5 a.m., confident that we had all the best sites and that our publicity machine (financed by the small amounts that could be raised by dances and similar functions) had far outstripped our opponents. In fact, within a few hours, there wasn't a Barratt poster in sight. As students went to the booths to vote, the bearded face of Alan Reay looked down on them from every point. Mine had all been obliterated or defaced. Loudspeaker cars roamed the streets urging everybody to vote for Reay. Eager groups of his supporters gathered round every polling station. To a visitor to Aberdeen that day, it must have seemed that the election was a one-horse race. A horse by the name of Reay.

Despite the fact that I had learned not to be overinfluenced by the loudest noise, I was deeply dejected. Defeat seemed likely. I might even end up bottom of the poll. It was a humbling experience, though no doubt a healthy one, and I began to realise for the first time the kind of agonies politicians must undergo at parliamentary elections, with so much more at stake. As we went to the Kirkgate bar that evening to wait for the result to be announced. I mentally rehearsed my little speech conceding defeat and congratulating the winner. What I hoped above all was that there would be no recount necessary. That would have prolonged the tension, I thought, past bearable limits.

And then it was all over. I had won. Not only that – it was almost a landslide, with nearly three times as many votes as my nearest rival and almost a clear majority over the other four candidates put together. It was one of the most exciting moments of my life and it opened for me a door into a whole new world.

A few days after the celebrations were over and the euphoria had passed, I met my friend, the late Kenneth Allsop, who, like Malcolm Muggeridge, had been Rector of Edinburgh University. I asked him how he had enjoyed his term of office there.

'Mike,' he said, 'I hate to tell you this, but those were the unhappiest three years of my life.'

The elation fell away from me then like rain off an oilskin, but my fears of sharing Ken's unhappy experiences were soon to prove unfounded. I have to thank Edward Wright, as much as anyone, for this. As Principal and vice-Chancellor, he could have made my introduction to office extremely difficult for me – as other Principals in other places had done for other Rectors. After all, I hardly knew my way around the university, I had no room of my own, nor even a desk, and I was certainly ignorant of the machinery of university government. In fact, he went out of his way to smooth my path and to give me the basic facilities I needed – partly because he is a kindly man, largely because he really has the students' interests at heart and has long been a champion of their cause.

My first job was to appoint an Assessor – a man or woman who would sit with me as a member of the Court and who would have a sound knowledge of such things as Government Quinquennial strategies, the work of the University Grants Commission, the political and financial implications of student expansion, staffing, accommodation and much else besides. I had promised that my Assessor would be a student and I set about taking soundings among all sections, both students and staff, to find the right person for a job that was becoming increasingly onerous. Among those I talked to was Norman Macdonald, soon to retire as President of the SRC (which had backed my opponent, Tom Tait, in the election). Norman, an MA honours graduate studying for an M Ed degree, had made a special study of Scottish Universities in the nineteenth century and confessed to having 'a somewhat old-fashioned (and perhaps reactionary) view of the dignity and of the supreme authority of the Court'. Yet I knew him to be a progressive thinker, conscious as I was of the need for change in the developing pattern of higher education.

This is how he saw the role of the person I was looking for: 'The position of Assessor is going to be a hard one, and whoever is appointed will have to be a strong and capable person, able to handle the problems of acting as the link between the Court and the students. It would also be virtually essential that he have some detailed knowledge of the relationship between the University and the students and the development of this relationship over the past few years because, as you are no doubt aware, the attitude of students towards the University has changed greatly, and their involvement in and knowledge of the University demands a level of performance and competence far beyond that acceptable in the past.'

I had been told that Jenny Hunt – daughter of a former Rector, Lord Hunt – who at the time had been Lady President of the Union, had declined Jo Grimond's offer to be his Assessor because she was not confident of her ability to do the job, as she did not feel that she had the experience or the temperament to enable her to stand up to the pressures involved. Jo Grimond finally chose another graduate, Ken Chew, who proved to have all the qualities that Norman had outlined.

My inclination was to select a woman student, to redress a little the imbalance of the sexes on the Court. I was also looking for someone who would remain at the university for the three years of my own stay, which set me searching among the medical students. In the end I plumped for Norman, a choice which has since been amply justified.

There was one more formal hurdle to be jumped – the Installation, an awesome ceremony at which I had to be robed before giving the traditional address. Now I am fairly well practised at giving public speeches – I suppose I average at least one a week in a normal year – yet the prospect of this one played havoc with my nervous system. I have a rule never to write a speech. I do not even use notes. But this time I had to break that rule (for one thing, the Press were demanding hand-outs in advance) and this is what emerged from my hesitant typewriter.

'I stand before you naked. Starkers. And even these splendid robes cannot hide the fact.

'If you glance down the list of previous Rectors of this ancient university, you will see that most of them had so many academic handles to their names that I wonder the University Press did not run out of type. They will have no such problem with the newly elected incumbent of this great office.

'Now you may think that this nakedness of mine makes my appearance in this hallowed hall of learning indecent, not to say obscene. Worse still, I happen to be a professional reporter – and we all know what that means: a mangler of the English language, as any Professor of Eng. Lit. will tell you.

'You know the sort of stuff we're supposed to write. "A weeping mother sobbed through her tears last night as she cried out for her baby." Or, "the striker propelled the leather spheroid beyond the upright." Despite that, some of us believe we know a thing or two about communication, about transmitting information and ideas to other men's minds. Learning is dependent on communication and so it is in this area that I timorously suggest a professional may have something to offer you.

'A rather precious and puritanical student the other day

was appalled to see his uncle entering a house of ill repute in Aberdeen. He tackled him about it later. "Uncle how could you – and you a respectable married man?"

' "Well, it's like this", said his uncle. "The grudging acquiescence o' your Aunt Matilda is no' to be compared wi' the enthusiastic co-operation o' a proper whore."

'As your Rector for the next three years, I pledge you my enthusiastic co-operation in striving for, among other things, better communication within the university and between the university and the world outside.

'For thousands of years, the imparting of knowledge and of intelligent opinion was cruelly restricted to The Few – to the Platonic Academy, perhaps, or to the laboriously penned manuscripts of a handful of scholars.

'And then along came printing. It was one of the greatest revolutions, the greatest leaps forward, in human history. At last there was a means of communicating with thousands rather than scores of people. At last learning could be made available to more than a tiny elite.

'Yet how was printing welcomed? "Thou hast most traitorously corrupted the youth of the realm in erecting a grammar school", says the rebel Jack Cade to the Lord Say in Shakespeare's *Henry the Sixth*, "and whereas, before, our forefathers had no other books but the score and the tally, thou hast caused printing to be used, and, contrary to the King, his crown, and dignity, thou hast built a paper mill."

'You know, people are still saying that kind of thing today – though they say it about television rather than printing. You have heard, I'm sure, those quasi-intellectuals at smart parties who say, "I never see television. We don't have a set in the house." They might as well boast that there are no books in their homes, that they never read. The analogy, I think, is fair. Television, after all, is a form of publishing – probably the most effective form – which is why, by the way, I am constantly sued for libel rather than slander.

'But to return for a moment to printing. The effectiveness of this great tool of communication was increased a hundred-fold by the arrival of the photograph. Man's awareness of his own world, his ability to share knowledge, was immeasurably improved. Among other things, a new style of popular journalism was born, with a new dimension, and as professional skills in the use of this medium matured, so did the opportunities for mass education.

'The adjective "popular", of course, is regarded by some as a synonym for "trivial" or "superficial", though goodness knows why it should be. Simple language – common language, if you like – is in my view infinitely to be preferred to the multisyllables and tortuous phraseology of what often passes for a "learned" paper. The art of communicating on any topic – whether it be Life itself or the price of porridge – demands the use of easily understood words and is greatly heightened by skilful illustration. Thus, my favourite description of the objects of pictorial journalism – of printed words and photographs – is to be found not in a textbook in the library at King's, but in what might be called a "publisher's blurb" for the now defunct *Life* magazine. It is this: "To see life; to see the world; to eyewitness great events; to watch the faces of the poor and the gestures of the proud; to see strange things – machines, armies, multitudes, shadows in the jungle and on the moon; to see man's work – his paintings, towers and discoveries; to see things thousands of miles away, things hidden behind walls and within rooms, things dangerous to some; to see the women that men love and many children; to see and take pleasure in seeing; to see and be amazed; to see and be instructed."

'Now that was written, by a strange coincidence, at a time when exciting experiments were under way with yet another, scientifically much more advanced technique of communication – the technique of television which in turn brought about the demise, 35 years later, of *Life* magazine itself and of others like it. Today, television provides the means "to see and be instructed". In a worldwide (not to say nationwide) sense, television is the most powerful instrument of education – yes, and of art and of entertainment. At a single moment in time, hundreds of millions of people may be informed of historic happenings, their eyes opened, their minds broadened.

'Despite the potency of this medium for those of you who would learn and those who would teach, I have heard it dismissed as a technical novelty; as a machine which cuts a deep swathe through the field of ignorance yet leaves the edges untouched; as no more than a mirror of phoney "images" created by public relations and advertising executives. Even a certain Mr Ustinov, giving his Rectorial address to a lesser university somewhere south of here, attempted to encourage this notion. "The reflection in the glass", he said, "has become more important than the man himself. Every gesture, every inflection, is studied in the light of the popularity it will bring. The malaise is everywhere, for very slowly the old decencies, the old hypocrisies, the old habits are surrendering to the technological novelty which surrounds us, and which changes every day." You will note the pejorative use of the word "popularity", the apparent reluctance to welcome change, which I trust is not shared here in Aberdeen.

'Nobody in his right mind would deny that we can seek out bad television like we can read a bad book; make a bad television programme like we can make a bad rectorial address. But this is in no sense to deny the immense power for good of the medium, and I would put it to you that a man whose job is to teach should learn to use these modern techniques as he learned to speak, to read and to write. And if he learns in a good school, he will understand that to communicate serious ideas does not require endless verbosity, unrelieved by visual excitement. Discussion of an issue is not necessarily superficial if it is brief, nor trivial if it is entertaining. In his time, cartoonist David Low was often able to say more about the fundamental political issues of the day with a few bold strokes of his brush than you would find in a whole volume of *Hansard*.

'Now you may think that I am preaching to the converted this morning. This university, after all, has done more than most in recent years to use television as an aid to teaching and, increasingly, to the exchange of ideas within its walls. But I am suggesting that we might make much greater use of it – that we might look to the day when our libraries are complemented and extended by shelves of Videotape cassettes which students might study in their own rooms, just as today they study books.

'Am I making an improper suggestion? Recording lectures with visual aids would require lecturers who had acquired some skill as – and here's a dirty word for you – "performers". But what is the objection to that? They are required now to write legibly if they use chalk on a blackboard, to speak without a stammer, to project their voices – to be performers, in fact. And increasingly, in matters of staff selection, there are demands that they be professional performers.

'Increasingly, too, today's universities must concern themselves with many aspects of student life which are outside the purely academic sphere but which directly concern students' ability to learn. Mental health, for instance, is closely connected with the price of a hot meal in the Refectory or the provision of suitable accommodation in Halls of Residence. And our ability to secure satisfactory facilities, paid for out of the public purse, depends on our ability to persuade the public of our need. You may think that is a tiresome fact, but it *is* a fact and it brings us back to that other dirty word, our "image".

'How are we to set about persuading the electorate, and through them government, that students deserve and require higher grants, that more resources are required for building student accommodation, that expansion can mean destruction without adequate facilities? By writing memoranda to the University grants Committee, perhaps? By muttering into our academic beards about cheap Press distortion of student life? I think not. If there is a substantially popular view that all students are drink-sodden drug-addicted layabouts who would insult our beloved Queen at the drop of a mortarboard, then we must get up off our hind legs and do something to put the record straight – by using, skilfully, the very techniques which others would employ to destroy us.

'It was a government White Paper, of all things, that most recently expounded a view which I think we should all like to see publicised as widely as possible. The Secretary of State's *Framework for Expansion* in education revealed that the government "consider higher education valuable for its contribution to the personal development of those who pursue it; at the same time they value its continued expansion as an investment in the nation's human talent in a time of rapid social change and technological development".

'And so say all of us. But how do we say it? How do we communicate that attitude to the electorate of a great democracy? I suggest that we learn to use the one medium that can effectively reach those millions so that they can "see and be instructed".'

CHAPTER EIGHT

Ideals and Exploration

I HELPED to win the war by joining the Army Cadet Force at school. Being sharp-eyed with a rifle and always keeping my boots brightly polished, I rose rapidly to the rank of Lance-Corporal. And then the war ended, thankfully robbing me of the chance of glory on the battlefield.

They wouldn't even have me for National Service after that. When I had to go for my medical, in January 1946, the nation was still in a state of euphoria about peace. The fighting was over and Churchill's grim warnings of menace from behind the Iron Curtain were still rumblings of a tired old man. It seemed clear that conscription would be ended any day and the Army medical boards were turning down more young men than they accepted. I was among them. Grade C3 they said I was, based as far as I could tell on my agreeing with the medical officer that I occasionally had stomach ache.

But if the patriotic brandishing of arms was lost to me as a way of expressing youthful idealism, there were other ways – like standing on soap boxes on the street corners of Glasgow, proclaiming the great cause of world government. (I had read *The Anatomy of Peace* and it had bowled me over.) I carried that particular torch, too, into the staid chamber of the Glasgow Parliamentary Debating Society, where I sat as the Independent member for Stafford, which happened to be the only constituency available. Although I was passionate about the cause of global peace, you will see that I was hardly the most rebellious of youths – which is why, perhaps, it was harder than it might have been for me as a father to tune into the same wavelength as my own teenage sons and daughters when their turn came to put the world to rights.

However, I tried, and that was one reason why, in the

television series *Personal Choice*, I decided to interview that most beautiful girl Marianne Faithfull, who at that time (it was 1968) seemed to represent a great number of young people who were questioning the whole basis of our society. I wanted to try to understand what people like her were seeking from life, what they wanted to change in the community and what to put in its place. By a strange coincidence, Henry Williamson (author of one of my best-loved books, *Salar the Salmon*) came into the studios for a recording the same afternoon – the coincidence being that both Henry and Marianne, representing wholly different generations, shared a fascination for the mythology of Lucifer. Again and again in our conversation, Marianne described her feelings in terms of light.

'A hundred years ago', she told me, 'a person in a flying saucer looking down at this planet would have seen a dark planet. Now they see a whole planet that is lit, great cities lit up' (she opened her arms to the usual battery of bulbs above us in the studio) 'lit-lit-lit-lit-lit, all over the place, light. It's not for nothing. It means something that we live in light now. In our minds we're not in light, we're not at all, but we must be getting nearer, the things we're finding out are so fantastic.'

I liked that, both the imagery and the optimism. Yet there was darkness, too . . .

'There are some people who are so poor and have no food and their children have no food: how can anyone expect them to think about eternity or life or perfection? They haven't got a chance, they just haven't got a hope in hell. If only people were not hungry and cold, if people didn't live all in one room, if children really could be happy – and they're the only people who really can be happy.'

But how did Marianne, well-heeled and well-fed, pursue her private quest for perfection? Her answers distressed me at the time. Four years later, I was still hearing them in my mind as some of the most tragic I ever heard.

She had been talking about Huxley's *Doors of Perception* and she went on, 'That is what drugs are. They're doors. We should be able to be in a state where we don't need cigarettes or drink or anything like that at all, or marijuana. But something like LSD – if it wasn't meant to happen it wouldn't have been invented somehow. I think it was important. I know so many people who, before they took LSD, were such a drag. They took LSD and they really opened up.'

She talked of drugs providing 'the little cracks' through which she could see . . . 'something like God, something calming, no delusion. You can go into a garden and you see the garden and you see the colours enhanced and this is where you get the difference between people who take drugs and people who don't. The state we should be in is perfection and the reason that we're here is to find it'.

But what did Marianne find? The very antithesis of a state of perfection. Inevitably (that's to say, I thought it was inevitable, though the drug lobby would dispute it) she was later to be found in a clinic, fighting for a life she had come perilously close to destroying, desperately trying to cure an addiction to that most pernicious drug, heroin.

I had some idea of what she was going through, because I had observed it in others during the course of many film reports I had made during the late sixties about the drug problem. I knew that the withdrawal symptoms were worse than most human beings could endure, which was why the addiction units had such a high failure rate and so many patients went back on the hard stuff, condemned to die at an early age.

I think the most pathetic sight I ever came across was of a 16-year-old girl in a Birmingham hospital. Beautiful she was, with a porcelain face. Instead of entering an addiction unit, she had agreed to her doctor's plan to put her in an ordinary hospital ward and make her unconscious for a period of weeks. Thus, during the most harrowing of the withdrawal phase, she was in a coma, fed intravenously and unaware of the tortures her body was undergoing. The treatment seemed to be working. When I saw her, she was beginning to regain consciousness. There was promise in that delicate face of happiness ahead, forged out of hopeless depravity. And then the sledgehammer comment :

'I fear the worst', said the doctor. 'When she is cured and leaves here, there is nowhere for her to go except home, no power vested in me to protect her from her own family. Her father is an alcoholic and her brother a heroin addict. She will not be able to resist the pressures they will put on her to go back on drugs.'

Not for the first time, my own emotions became mixed up with my professional duties as a reporter. I felt that I ought to be involved, that I ought to offer her a home with us when the hospital treatment was complete. In the end, I did not. My fear that she might lapse back into drugs and somehow pollute our own family life proved greater than my anxiety to give her a fresh chance. She has been on my conscience ever since.

As our coverage, on film and in the studio, of the great drug debate developed, my own objectivity became dented. The argument that soft drugs like marijuana were virtually harmless, and certainly preferable to alcohol or nicotine, sent shivers down my spine. I did not, of course, believe that marijuana necessarily led to hard drugs, but I could not get out of my mind all those junkies whose road to self-destruction had begun with marijuana. Some told me how they had been persuaded to experiment with a jab of heroin while they were in a euphoric state, perhaps at a party, as a result of taking marijuana. Others recalled (in their brief periods of lucidity) how marijuana had given them the desire to seek other pleasures, other escapes, through different types of drugs, leading from the soft to the hard variety.

I was asked by several headmasters at the time to give lectures on drugs to their fourth, fifth and sixth formers. Clearly the object was to dissuade their pupils from taking drugs, but I took the view that to 'preach' to them would do more harm than good. Creating a taboo out of the drug scene was likely to have the effect of arousing curiosity and a desire to experiment. That's why I confined myself to reporting what I had seen and the junkies I had met in various addiction centres, leaving the pupils to draw their own conclusions without any moralising from me. I could usually tell whether I'd 'got through' to a young audience by the questions they would ask me and at one school in particular I remember being convinced that the youngsters were impressed – until, at the end of the session, the headmaster rose to thank me for coming along. Gathering his gown around him and wagging an admonitory finger at his pupils, he thundered, 'Let what you have heard be a lesson to you', and I knew that I might as well not have bothered, as the pupils' sympathy visibly turned to resentment and rebellion.

Behind much of the drug-taking was a genuine, normal and healthy desire to explore the meaning of life, to seek a kind of liberty from conventional social restraints, to open those doors that Marianne had talked about. But surely there can be no short cut in the pursuit of understanding; drugs, dangerous as they are, can be no chemical substitute for the sustained exercise of the mind. They are the products of a fundamentally lazy generation.

'Liberty of body and soul' was an aspiration that Edna O'Brien had reflected in her novels and that was why she became my second *Personal Choice*. Here was no lazy mind!

'I think I am hooked', she told me, 'on liberty for myself and for other people. I think what I mean by liberty is perhaps to be rid of many of the things that assail us – like making money, being loved, being a respectable person. I find more and more that a great amount of falseness and waste goes into our lives. We communicate in a way that is, to me anyhow, so untruthful.

'Rodin said of his whole life that he thought of it as one great long working day, and I consider that liberty, because it is a man who is aspiring to the highest things. What I fear about our lives is that if our lives were about to end – which God forbid – we would be impatient with ourselves for the way we tie ourselves down. Children have a natural freedom. As children we are free. We are spontaneous and we are open people. And then we go to school and we get indoctrinated by our parents and by our teachers and by the newspapers and by our so-called seniors, about behaviour, when most of what we are taught about behaviour is to put on mask after mask after mask.'

How are we to take off those masks, to find that kind of liberty? When I was a teenager, I thought I found a clue in the pages of J. W. Dunne's *Nothing Dies*. I tried, and have done ever since, to think of Time as three-dimensional – not as something which 'flows', as our conscious minds tell us, from past to present to future. All three are 'here and now'. I am not aware of dreaming very often, but if I do, there is often this fusion. Elements in a dream sequence will include incidents of the past, an almost conscious awareness of things present (some call it 'think-dreaming') and a third element which is at the time puzzling but which later proves to be a glimpse into the future.

Communicating this concept is particularly difficult – Dunne was rather better at it! – because I am saddled with words like 'later' and 'at the time'. Trying to break out of the shackles of ingrained beliefs about Time flowing from one point to another opens some doors of perception for me. It makes sense of 'Life after Death': there is no 'after' and therefore no Death. Mix that concept with the Schweitzer ethic of 'Reverence for Life', stir well, and you have some important ingredients of Liberty and Perception.

CHAPTER NINE
News Nationwide

A PAGE from the diary of a typical working day . . .

Tuesday, April 10, 1973:

Up at six. I have to write my column for the local *Bracknell Times* and deliver it before going to the studios. What shall I write about this week? At the kitchen table, I sit in front of the typewriter and that blank sheet of paper stares back at me. I recall the story of the journalist who locked himself in his room, determined to write the piece that would make his name as a great writer. After a few days, his friends broke the door down and found him lying on the floor, surrounded by hundreds of pieces of paper all of which had the words typed on them: 'Never since the death of Jesus Christ.' And nothing more.

I am still sitting at the typewriter. I have been writing this column every week for two years now and I wonder why. The payment amounts to peanuts and most of it goes to the Inland Revenue, anyway, so what possessed me to take it on? A desire, which I sometimes think is masochistic, to contribute to our village life. I am pledged to the building of a new hall, particularly to cater for the needs of the old people who constitute over 15 per cent of the village's population, as well as helping local 'good causes' like the hospital for mentally handicapped children. The column, I remember thinking at the time they asked me to do it, would be a useful vehicle for promoting these and other efforts. It has become a burden I could well do without.

I am still sitting at the typewriter. How much better it would be if I were out on the golf course, playing a few holes before going to work. I'm getting flabby again and need the exercise to tighten up. As it is, I haven't held a club in my hands for

This is a picture of a male chauvinist pig. Who does he think he is, with a great smirk on his face, presiding over a cattle market? How degrading to womankind!
Beauty contests have come in for much criticism in recent years, especially from the Women's Libbers, but I can see nothing degrading in a pretty face and a beautiful body. Nor have I anything but praise for the girls who are prepared to parade their physical talents in the cause of charity.
What pictures like this really mean is that some money has been raised for a village community centre, or for giving some succour to poor lonely old people, or for providing facilities to aid the mentally handicapped, the crippled, the orphaned . . .
My only complaint with most beauty contests is that they persist with the fiction of awarding points for qualities like 'personality' and 'charm' and even, sometimes, 'intelligence'. The compère asks: 'Is it true that your hobbies are riding and photography?' The contestant answers 'Yes' – and the judges are supposed to deduce something about her grey matter from that.

Jim Whalley

weeks now. Haven't had any 'time off', come to that, for a long time, with weekend work for radio (like *Gardeners' Question Time*), writing and other television programmes outside my normal *Nationwide* commitments. I enjoy working and I think I have a constitution of steel but there must be limits to anyone's physical, mental and nervous stamina. Am I stretching those limits? I ought to take a holiday. But when? I leaf through the diary and fail to find a single week without commitments to programmes, to the university or to charity events of one sort or another. Joan joins me at the breakfast table (it's school holiday time, so the children are mercifully still in bed) and reads my thoughts. 'You must get away', she says.

'I can't.'

'You must. There's nothing so vital that you can't cancel it. Tell them in the office today that you're going away next month. If they don't like it, that's their problem.' Women have an irritating habit of making these things sound so simple.

I am still sitting at the typewriter. I must stop chattering and day-dreaming. Maybe I should just ring up the *Times* office and tell them there'll be no column this week. They could put in a line that 'Michael Barratt is on holiday' or something of the sort. No, I know that won't do. I've never missed a column, never missed a single day's work in my life and I'm not going to start now. I think that's a proud boast; maybe it's a foolish one. However, it's me and I won't change, so let's get down to it. Time is running out. I remember a conversation with my friend Adam in the pub last night. Yes, that's it. At last I begin to pound away on the keys . . .

'One cautionary tale, coming up.

'It concerns hundreds of shopkeepers, publicans, businessmen of all kinds in this area who have recently become the targets of a particularly shabby attempt to get them to part with their money.

'The case of Adam Mackinnon is typical, though it includes an extra twist which I had not come across before.

'Mr Mackinnon, who is the proprietor of the Cottage Inn at Maidens Green near Bracknell, received a phone call recently telling him that the telephone directory was being reorganised to simplify its production and asking him if he would like a fresh entry in the Yellow Pages section. He replied that, to keep things simple, he would leave his entries as they were, thank you very much.

'A few days later, in his own words, "I received a bill for £10.50 for my entry in the directory. What a racket! I'm going to write back and tell them I refuse to pay it."

'It all seemed very odd to me and unlike the method of selling space in the Yellow Pages, so I asked him to show me the "bill". It turned out to be a form which has become very familiar indeed and which I thought we had satisfactorily exposed in *Nationwide*.

'The form certainly looks like an invoice – as it is meant to do. It is headed *National Business and Professional Trades Directory*. It carries the same details of address and telephone number as the Post Office directory and in heavy black type are the words:

' "Payment to be made to Commercial and Trades Directories, 13 Royal Parade (rear of), Blackheath, London SE13."

'It informs Mr Mackinnon that the "proposed details of entry" are in light type under the classification "Inns" and that he should "please attach any corrections and return with remittance advice". Further, "if payment for this entry is made within ten days, deduct five per cent" from the total cost of £10.50.

'There are two copies of this form which look like an invoice, one marked "please retain this for your records", the other "please return with remittance".

'I asked Mr Mackinnon to put his glasses on and read every word on that form, as I would beg you to do if you have received one through the post recently. For there, at the foot, are the words, "Publishing conditions overleaf. This is not a claim for payment".

'And overleaf, it says this:

' "Commercial and Trades Directories intend to publish the National Business and Professional Trades Directory 1973 for the United Kingdom. Distribution will be world-wide at no charge to Public Libraries, Trade Commissioners, Embassies, and to prospective buyers on an applied for basis.

' "This is a solicitation and not an assertion of a right to

Carnivals, fêtes, dog shows, spring fairs, autumn fayres, jumble sales . . . There are few week-ends free of them. Each New Year I resolve to say 'no' to all invitations to open them, yet there always seems a compelling reason to break the resolution. Next year, however, I shall be unmoved by all entreaties, however needy the charity. I think.

payment. Upon payment Commercial and Trades Directories will publish the National Business and Professional Trades Directory with the Payee's entry as overleaf or as corrected by the Payee."

'You see, it's *not* an invoice, however much it looks like one.

'The careful wording keeps it within the bounds of legality. But I wonder how many people it has fooled in these parts, people who think they are committed to paying for a directory entry they can't remember asking for.

'In Mr Mackinnon's case, the telephoned solicitation for an entry in the Yellow Pages, properly made according to normal business practice, was an unfortunate coincidence which added to his confusion.

'Let no one else hereabout be confused.'

To complete the column, I add a few paragraphs about the local Operatic Society, of which I'm President – a ridiculous position as I'm tone deaf and musically ignorant, and one I could well do without. What possessed me to take it on?

What a beautiful day it is! The daffodils are in full bloom all round the house and I envy Joan who can enjoy our green acres all day long, far from the madding crowd. She no doubt is envying me because in contrast to her daily routine of housework, feeding the hens, meeting the same people in the same village shop, I shall have a day of fresh challenges, fresh experiences, fresh faces.

The papers arrive and I read them with tonight's programme in mind. It seems a pretty thin day for news – the usual industrial unrest, a soldier killed in Northern Ireland, constituency reports on the new county councils' election campaigns, nothing that we have not covered again and again in *Nationwide*.

The post arrives. I wish it wouldn't. There's a recorded delivery packet of prosecutions for parking – I'm known as an 'alleged high offender' – and one of those buff envelopes from the Inspector of Taxes, which I re-address unopened to my accountant because I haven't the nerve to read the contents. There's a bundle of letters from the hanging brigade, fuming about a piece I wrote in a recent column for the *Weekly News* in which I suggested that human life was sacred and that neither judge nor jury should have the power to take it away.

Then there's the inevitable letter which begins 'I always enjoy *Nationwide*, particularly the way you champion good causes' and goes on to ask for my help in finding a council house for a poor family. How does the writer discover my home address? Simply by marking the envelope 'Michael Barratt, Berkshire'. There's no time to answer any of the mail. I have a quick bath, change into a suit (how I hate suits), shout at the children that it's long past time they were up, kiss Joan and promise her that yes, really, I will try to get my hair cut at lunchtime, and set off for the office.

On the way along the M4 I switch radio channels to catch all the news bulletins, but there is still nothing which prompts an idea for tonight's programme. After nearly four years of *Nationwide*, 50 minutes a night, fresh topics are hard to come by. What a voracious medium we work in!

I'm in the office just before 10.30. The usual bedlam. There are about 25 of us in one room, secretaries pounding away on typewriters, researchers shouting down telephones, production assistants listening to playbacks of films and Videotape recordings . . .

'Morning, Mike', says John Morrell who is editing today's show. 'Any ideas? There's nothing much in the news prospects, but Bob Wellings is working on an item about London traffic with the GLC party leaders which should run to 15 minutes or so.'

I search for ideas in my mail. There are 94 letters for me today. A couple are abusive, a girl of six says she is in love with me and wants my autograph, six charity organisations ask me to open their fêtes, but the rest are mostly suggestions for film stories which I pass on to our Forward Planning team. There's nothing for today, except for a letter from a man who says he objects to the way I often end a programme with the words 'See you tomorrow'. I'll keep that one beside me. It might come in useful if I have a few seconds to fill on the air.

Let's hope some bright ideas emerge on 'the circuit'. That's at 10.45 when we discuss prospects with the editors of regional programmes in Glasgow, Newcastle, Leeds, Manchester, Birmingham, Norwich, Cardiff, Bristol, Plymouth, Southampton and Belfast. From most of them today the message is

Aware from my own youth of the importance of village life, I plunged into fund-raising for a new hall in our own village of Binfield in Berkshire. For a start, we ran a Donkey Derby at our home – which meant months of effort for a minimal return (about £200 profit, as I remember). Yet the sheer hard graft brought a longer-term reward. Impressed by the evidence of communal self-help, individuals and local authorities offered their own contributions and within two years we had around £30,000 in the kitty.

Keystone-Press pictures by Chris Ware

basically 'Nothing doing'. They're all concentrating heavily on coverage of the county council election campaigns in their own programmes, but otherwise the cupboard is bare.

John begins to build a running order. We know it will change several times before transmission but it provides a skeleton to work on and apportions responsibilities to production assistants and presenters: Sue Lawley and Bob Wellings are with me today. The first 20 minutes, for viewers in London and the South-East, are sewn up – the GLC debate taking up most of the time, plus a light-hearted film which Christopher Rainbow has made about a man who has given his wife a cinema for her birthday. That should provide a necessary contrast to the heavy stuff.

For Part Two, seen throughout the country, we are committed to an interview with Mark Bonham Carter, chairman of the Community Relations Commission. His appearance on the programme last night brought an avalanche of phone calls from viewers and our Editor, Michael Bunce, decided that we must have Mr Bonham Carter back in the studio to answer some of their questions and complaints. In addition, we have Michael Molyneux at our Legal Desk, explaining the laws about liability when people have accidents caused by the carelessness of others. Two good public service items there, but the programme is looking rather heavy. We need some light relief if we are to hold viewers' interest: there's a limit to the serious fare they can absorb, or want to, at this time in the evening. John goes to the viewing theatre to see what films are available. Bob has retired to a quiet room to study research material about London's traffic problem. I watch a recording of last night's show to take notes of questions arising from the race relations debate.

12.10 p.m. A message comes over the 'tannoy' system from our news service: 'Reports are coming in of a British plane crash in Switzerland. No further details.' Ron Neil, senior producer of the day, phones the Press Association to check on the story, but there is no additional information.

12.20. 'Reports from Switzerland suggest that there are no casualties in the plane crash. Believed to be a charter flight.'

Flying accidents have been much in the news of late. There

have been alarming, or perhaps needlessly alarmist, stories about pilot fatigue and other factors affecting safety in the air which have led to public disquiet. We begin to sniff a topic for tonight. There's not enough to go on yet, but our Antennae are out.

12.30. 'All feared dead in the Swiss plane crash. Reports from Basle, unconfirmed, say that the plane was operated by Invicta Airlines out of Bristol and that it crashed into a mountainside near the airport.'

Suddenly it's action stations throughout the office. Reporter Bernard Falk walks in 'Ah, Bernard!' says John Morrell, back from viewing, 'can you go straight out to the airport? Get on the first plane going to Switzerland. Aileen, fix a car right away to take Bernard to Heathrow will you love? Margaret, check on flights to Basle, Zurich or Geneva. Anne, organise some money to be waiting for Bernard at the airport bank. Phone in before you leave, Bernard, so that we know where you're going. We'll know a bit more about the strength of the story by then.'

John is working on a newsman's hunch, gambling on a trained instinct that tells him we have a major story on our hands. He's right. As the news tapes begin to come in, we learn that there were 145 people aboard the plane, that it crashed in a blizzard and that – most tragic of all – 63 of the passengers were believed to be women from the village of Axbridge (total population 1,000) in Somerset, on a day's shopping trip. Lunch forgotten, we all contribute what we can to filling in the pieces of a jigsaw which must be assembled by six o'clock. I ring my friend Harry Chandler, chairman of the Tour Operators' Study Group, to secure names and phone numbers and facts about the Invicta company. Other members of the team search for expert air correspondents who can be interviewed about the background to the crash and air safety in general, check on the record of Vanguard aircraft, consult our colleagues in Bristol about the passenger list, order maps of the Basle district from our graphics department and so on. As the story builds up, it seems to centre on that little village, so many of whose wives and mothers may have been killed. Deputy Editor Stuart Wilkinson gets in touch with one of our film crews, working at the time with director Bill Jones and reporter James

Hogg in the Cheltenham area, and diverts them to Axbridge. There's just a chance that if they can get there in time, they might be able to produce 30 seconds or so on film tonight. We hear from Bernard Falk that he's on his way to Zurich. Phone lines are booked to the Swiss television studios there so that he can report 'live' into the programme.

By four o'clock, John has to pull together everybody's efforts, though there is still serious confusion in the news tapes about details of the crash. What we laughingly call a 'notional running order' goes up on the board in the office. It looks like this:

'Headlines. (Mike + Sue).
Mike introduces Ruby's Birthday film.
Bob intros GLC debate.
Mike intros weather.
Mike intros Crash; interview John Norman in Bristol; phone call to James Hogg in Axbridge; phone call to Bernard Falk in Zurich; interview Invicta man if poss. in studio; Mike and Bob on safety of flying + statistics + Andrew Wilson interview.
Mike intros Legal Desk + Michael Molyneux.
Sue intros Hilbre Island film.
Mike interviews Bonham Carter.
Crash update.
Goodnight.

We begin to write as many of the 'links' as we can. I produce the following headline sequence:

MIKE: Good evening. The decimated village. We report tonight from Axbridge in Somerset, whose population was a thousand – until this morning, when the Vanguard crashed in Switzerland with 77 villagers on board.

SUE: Also tonight, the problems of race relations in Britain. Mark Bonham Carter, chairman of the Community Relations Commission, returns to our studio to answer your questions.

MIKE: And, from our Legal Desk, advice on your rights in
the event of an accident. All that and more after your
own news nationwide.

As the last hour or so ticks away before transmission time, the crash story develops its drama. The mental picture that stays with me all afternoon is of the fathers and children at Bristol airport, waiting, waiting for news of the womenfolk. As more and more news tapes contradict each other, so their agony must be heightened. I am convinced that, if only for their sakes, we must transmit every morsel of corroborated information we can lay our hands on. And for others who plan similar trips in the coming months, we must examine as fully as possible the standards of safety on both independent charters such as this one and scheduled flights by the major airlines. However, I know that there is a dangerously thin line to be trodden between that kind of coverage as a public service and the exploitation of a tragic accident as a means of titillating some viewers. 'Let's try as far as we can', I say to Bob and Sue, 'to avoid using adjectives tonight.'

At 5.40, the three of us move down to the studio. I know we're in for a rough ride tonight because the news is changing minute by minute and we are far from sure what the main elements will turn out to be in the crash story.

At 5.50, less than ten minutes before we're due on the air, Editor Michael Bunce comes into the studio. 'I don't like the headlines', he says. 'I want them to be all about the air crash, delivered by Mike straight to camera. And I don't like that phrase "the decimated village". That means it has been reduced to a tenth. Not true. There's a rewrite on the way down.'

Two minutes to transmission and the new script lands on my desk. It begins, 'the village of tragedy'. Well, I don't like *that*! Michael agrees that I can change it, though there's no time to discuss what I might say instead. 'Stand by, studio,' says Leon the floor manager. 'Good luck, Mike, says director Alex Saward through my earpiece. 'Ten seconds', says Leon. 'Quiet, please.'

And we're on the air. Animated titles as usual. Then, 'cue Mike'.

'Good evening. The village hit by disaster. We report to-night from Axbridge in Somerset, whose population was a thousand until this morning when the Vanguard crashed in Switzerland with 63 villagers on board. Bernard Falk is in Switzerland to report on the latest news from the scene of the crash. And we'll also be looking into the recent history of air safety: the 59 crashes in the last 15 months, the 2,600 people killed in them, That's after your own news nationwide.'

The programme symbol spins to the last five seconds of music, the director tells the other regions to 'opt out', again it's 'cue Mike' on Camera One – and I suddenly realise that our first item is that lighthearted piece about an amusing birthday present. I effect a decidedly clumsy 'gear change' to the effect that 'happily not all today's news is distressing', and plough on with my introduction to 'Ruby's Birthday'.

After the film, Bob goes into his GLC discussion and I have 15 precious minutes in which to digest the latest tapes about the air crash, though it's still not clear whom I'll be talking to, about what. Bob ends his discussion and hands back to me as Aileen the production assistant in the gallery, beside the director, counts down in my ear: five, four, three, two . . . 'Now the weather nationwide', I say at precisely 6.20. The other regions are given one and a half seconds to 'opt in' to us again and we're away.

'Today has been a macabre one for me and most of my colleagues in *Nationwide* as we have tried to piece together the facts about the plane crash in the mountains of Switzerland near Basle. Hope and despair have fluctuated, as they must have done most tragically in the little Somerset village of Axbridge. At first, we heard that all the passengers were safe, then that they were all feared dead, then that an unknown number were thought to have survived.

'Among the passengers were 63 members of the Axbridge Women's Guild for whom the flight was to be a one-day shopping trip. We still don't know how many of them may be alive, though tonight we shall do our best to unravel the often conflicting and contradictory reports. In Switzerland now is Bernard Falk and I'm waiting for his call to tell us the latest news from there.

'I also want to ask Andrew Wilson how safe flying is now' (as I talk, Alex chirps up through the earpiece that we're going into an interview with John Norman in Bristol) 'in the light of a record of 59 civil aircraft crashing in the last 15 months, killing 2,620 people. I want to know more, too, about the safety record of Vanguard aircraft, about the weather conditions at Basle today, about the Invicta company and about the crew. But first, John Norman, let's begin at the beginning. Who was on the plane when it left Bristol this morning?'

I turn to the bank of monitors behind me and there is John all right, but not a sound passes his lips. That's a good start! But the technical problem is instantly solved and we continue the interview. As we do so, Alex tells me that the next sequence – a phone call from James Hogg in Axbridge – is out. Instead there's a call from Bernard in Zurich. But which phone? There are two on my desk. As I'm saying 'thank you, John', Alex shouts in my ear 'on 5491'. Turning to the camera, I say something about calling up Bernard Falk, lift up the phone – and, thank goodness, there he is on the end of the line. I know he has been there only an hour or so, yet he gives us a brilliant report, explaining the appalling weather conditions on the spot, the hazards of the rescue operation and the consequent pro-blems of securing reliable information about the numbers of dead and the survivors. Again, as we talk, Alex is telling me that the next item is to be a report by Christopher Rainbow about the history of the Invicta airline. Then Bernard is back on the line from Zurich with the first-hand account of a survivor. We have Invicta boss Hugh Kennard on the other phone and Andrew Wilson of the *Observer* beside me to talk about safety. In the middle of that, I'm told that we have a film report from James Hogg, shot in Axbridge a couple of hours earlier as the shocked villagers waited for news. 'Give me an earpull or a noserub', says Alex.

The films we show in each programme are operated from what's known as a telecine machine. It takes the machine eight seconds – or ten feet of film – to run up to the required speed. Thus, when I'm introducing a film report, the director needs to start the telecine machine exactly eight seconds before my final word. With a scripted introduction, he can make that calculation fairly easily and, as a further aid, his production assistant in the gallery 'counts me down', ten – nine – eight and so on, through my earpiece. However, if there is no script, as in this case, the director has to wait for a signal from me to start the machine. When I touch my ear, or my nose, that's the signal . . . From then on, I ad lib for precisely eight seconds until, with a bit of luck, the film appears on the screen.

After the Axbridge film, which includes a most moving interview with the Vicar's wife who should have been on the flight but changed her mind, I have another interview to conduct – this time with a travel agent in the Bristol studio. I've never heard of him before, but he contributes useful additional information about the circumstances of this particular charter trip. That 'notional running order' established earlier in the afternoon is now unrecognisable; we are responding, on air, to events as they happen. It's a great strain on the nervous system and the reserves of adrenalin, but I'm stimulated by the thought that we're doing a sound professional job with every member of our diverse team pulling out all the stops.

During the interview with the travel agent, I'm told that we are going on to the item with Mark Bonham Carter. I wonder if they realise that he is not in the studio. I plough on, hopefully, with the scripted words.

'Some of you watching now may well be among the dozens of people who rushed for their telephones during Nationwide last night when Frank Bough was discussing the subject of Race Relations. For instance' (there's a lot of scuffling around me in the studio, but no sign yet of my victim) 'Mrs Jeremy of Barnes, London, had this to say about Mr Mark Bonham Carter, chairman of the Community Relations Commission: "He intends the end of the Anglo-Saxon Race."

'And another caller who wouldn't leave his name said the BBC's attitude was a travesty, "telling people they had got to be fair to immigrants".'

As I come to the end of the introduction, Mr Bonham Carter nips into the chair beside me and we launch into what I hope appears a relaxed and reasoned discussion on this highly charged subject. But while we're debating the problems of black people in a predominantly white community, I'm still being fed with information about the air crash and, with a minute of programme time to go, I am back on the phone to Bernard for the latest news in Switzerland.

'Fifteen seconds to go', says Aileen. 'Ten . . .' I thank Bernard, turn to camera to say 'goodnight' to viewers. The symbol whirls, the music plays us out as the countdown reaches zero.

'Bloody marvellous!' says Alec in my ear. And suddenly I'm very tired.

I don't know precisely – and perhaps it's just as well – what effects the strains of live television for prolonged periods have on my system, though there is evidence that my pulse rate increases massively – not so much during the show as after it, when I've said 'goodnight'. All I know is that I need half an hour or so to unwind before I dare trust myself to drive the car home safely. I also need a glass of whisky. But just as I need that nip afterwards, I have a rule never to take a drink during the day before a programme. It is a rule I have never broken because I believe that even a glass of beer at lunchtime would be sufficient to take the edge off my voice and slow down my mental reactions. That may be codswallop, but it suits me to believe it!

So tonight, I flop into a chair in the hospitality room and sip my Scotch and join in the post mortem on the programme. There is general satisfaction that we have done a responsible, professional job and team morale is high. I think, too, about those people waiting for news at the airport and I hope we have given them at least some of the facts they were hungry for.

On my way home, I call in as usual at our 'local' (another unbroken ritual) and pick up a bottle of wine for dinner. Home at 8.30. Exhausted. I really have stretched myself to the limit today and I'm in danger of falling asleep over the meal as I recount the day's events to Joan and listen to her critique of the programme.

At 9.30 I'm ready for bed. The phone rings. 'Is that Michael Barratt of Nationwide? My name is So-and-so. I want to tell you that I usually enjoy your programmes, but tonight I was appalled by the way you reported the air accident. You were disgustingly over-emotional and I must protest.'

I could do without that. I am tempted to slam the phone down. How dare this woman intrude into my fleeting home life? But I say, 'Madam, I am sorry you don't approve of what we did tonight, but I can assure you it was done with good and honest intention. We felt that those villagers in particular wanted to be given every scrap of information about their wives and mothers that our team could garner. For myself, I have worked extremely hard all day to provide that service and I am now very, very tired.'

'I'm not concerned about how tired you are. I just want to say that your cheap emotionalism was disgusting and obscene.'

'Goodnight, madam.' I put the phone down.

It is time for bed.

CHAPTER TEN

Flights, Fights and Frights

MEMORY PLAYS strange, though not unwelcome tricks. Without either a diary or a scrapbook of press cuttings (both of which I have been too lazy to keep) my passport is the only aid to recollection and, as I flip through its crowded pages, I find myself looking back at happenings which were often harrowing at the time but now seem positively enjoyable.

There's the faded green stamp, for instance, which reads: '23.12.63 DDR'. Yes, I remember it well. East Germany. The Berlin Wall, that awful symbol of Man's inhumanity.

I had been told to go to West Berlin, where *Panorama* had set up 'live' cameras, to report on the one-way Christmas 'truce' which allowed West Berliners to pass through the Wall to visit the relatives in the East from whom they had been so long separated. Thick fog meant that I could not fly there direct; instead, I had to take a plane to Hamburg, then a train to Hanover, then another train which took us through that bitterly cold night across the border, into East Berlin and on to the West. At least, that was the idea. In fact, I got off the train at the wrong station.

In the Communist city I was lost – and not a little frightened. I could not speak a word of German (classical Greek and Latin at school had ill prepared me for travelling around Europe) and I could find nobody with even a smattering of English who could guide me to the other side. Sullen faces stared at me as I hopped on and off trains in a blind attempt to find my way to the station of the West. I wondered how many of them might be secret police. Perhaps I had read too many bad spy stories, but I expected at any moment to feel some heavy hand on my shoulder and to be whisked away to some Eastern detention camp. I could visualise the headlines back home: 'TV Man Vanishes Behind Iron Curtain.'

I still can't work out how I arrived in the West, but I did and joined our director, Dick Francis, at our outside broadcast position beside 'the hole in the Wall'. I went on the air that night standing in the freezing fog as West Berliners trailed through to meet their relatives and take them gifts like cabbages and other basics. There was no glitter and no joy, no goodwill under the surveillance of those trigger-happy Communist guards.

The next morning, Christmas Eve, was traumatic. For the Barratt family, Christmas has always been a time of great happiness, the only time that we can be assured of enjoying each other. Every one of us is crucial to the corporate delight. There is a ritual which demands that I go on a local pub crawl on Christmas Eve and pass my inhibitions through my bladder while Joan and the children make the mince pies, decorate the house and then settle down to the umpteenth showing of 'Rebecca' on the telly. The children (adults among them included) peel off for bed before I arrive home and Joan fills the stockings. In each is an apple, an orange, a paper trumpet, six chocolate pennies, crayons, and assorted plastic toys. I stumble home and insist on doing my Father Christmas act and placing the stockings on the end of all the beds.

'You'll fall down as usual and wake all the children', says Joan.

'Nonsense', I say, gathering up the stockings and starting uncertainly upstairs. Half way up, I trip over a step. Stocking fillings spew all over the place. The children wake up but pretend not to. I start again.

At the crack of Christmas dawn I pad round the bedrooms. 'What has Father Christmas brought you?' I ask them all. They maintain the charade. We have an early breakfast and set off for church. Home again, we gather round the tree and I dole out the presents. We have spent the last month or so laying false trails and false expectations so that each present may be a real surprise. We are, for one precious day, a family completely at peace with itself. We laugh together and overeat together and play games together. None of us ever goes out, nor would visitors – even the closest of friends – be allowed in.

We are our own world. We are happy.

Back to Berlin that Christmas Eve, 1963. The fog was still thick in the morning and all flights out of the airport were grounded. There was, it seemed, no possible means of my getting home. I was distraught and cursed myself for ever considering a job which showed every prospect of destroying family life. Hour after hour I sat in that departure lounge with Dick, willing myself home but helplessly staring at a blanket of fog. For me, then, the Berlin Wall, tensions between East and West, fears of a new war that might destroy the world, were of no consequence. It was my own little world that was at risk and I was frightened.

At long last the fog began to thin out. There was an announcement that a plane to Frankfurt was about to take off. We jumped at the chance of a couple of seats on it. Frankfurt wasn't home, by any means, but it was a step nearer. As we touched down at the international airport there, we saw a Qantas Boeing on the tarmac. 'I bet that's going to London', said Dick.

'If it is,' I said, 'we're going to be on it.'

We came near to breaking the world sprint record as we dashed across that apron and into the Arrivals building. 'Is that the London flight?' we blurted at the girl behind the Qantas desk. 'It is? Right, we want to be on it. Hold it for us, will you?' As we charged through to Departures, the girl was too startled to ask questions. She was on the phone, and a few minutes later, the door of that Boeing was opened for us to get aboard. It took less than ten minutes between our landing from Berlin and taking off in another plane for London, certainly the quickest turn-round I have ever effected.

Our family Christmas was saved. The ritual, more pagan I suppose than Christian, was preserved for another year and on Boxing Day we completed our custom by holding Open House, when all our friends are invited to a party which goes on from ten in the morning to some unearthly hour the next morning. That year, they all said the same thing:

'Congratulations on making it to the top. Travelling round the world for Panorama must be a wonderful experience. How I envy you!'

They couldn't understand, and I didn't try to tell them how, that Christmas, I'd have given all I possessed for a nine-to-five job as a bank clerk.

The feeling didn't last, of course. World travel and the opportunity to participate in historic events wherever they might happen, was as addictive as any drug. Within a few days I was happily on my way again.

In May, 1964, I was sent out to the Middle East with cameraman Nat Crosby, his assistant Frank Hodge and sound recordist John Hore. I was to be director as well as reporter, which was what I always wanted to do. I believed that, as a journalist, filming for television meant that I could use different tools of communication. Instead of a typewriter and the techniques of typographical display, I had a camera and the new dimension of moving pictures. And I wanted to use these tools my way. I wanted to say things sometimes with pictures and music or sound effects rather than with words. Directing my own reports gave me that opportunity. It was not a popular view in the production team, of course, but it sometimes prevailed if only because the severely limited programme budget would not stretch to more than four air fares on a long trip. (The need for economy had another, less welcome effect: it meant that once we had arrived in some far-flung spot, we would be asked to stay in the area for weeks on end, producing the maximum amount of material for one set of fares.)

Our first job on this trip was to cover the first major operation in constructing President Nasser's dream, the Aswan Dam, diverting the waters of the great River Nile. The ceremony was to be conducted by Nikita Khruschev, so it looked as though we had the elements of a strong report – spectacular pictures and two of the most controversial figures on the world stage. As soon as we arrived in Cairo, I put in an official bid for an interview with President Nasser. I knew the chances of his talking to a reporter from British television were slim and that I was probably at the end of a long queue of other reporters who had made the same request. To my astonishment, though, the reply was a pleasant, 'Of course. Why not?'

I was exultant. Here was promise of a major scoop. In the succeeding days I learned better. It was the Egyptian officials' way of getting us off their backs. I think every request we ever made during our stay in the United Arab Republic was met with those words, 'Why not?' They became the catchphrase of our trip.

Next morning, we were at the airport to board the Viscount of United Arab Airlines to fly to Aswan by way of Luxor. The ceremony was to be at 11.30, so we would have several hours to set up cameras in the best position on the site and carry out some on-the-spot research. And then those dreaded words came over the tannoy system: 'United Arab Airlines regret to announce a delay in the departure of their flight to Luxor and Aswan.' Yet again, an airport waiting room had become the scene of awful frustration. As the minutes and then the hours ticked away, the prospect grew of our missing the event we had come all that way, at such great expense, to film. 'Sorry, but the plane had a technical fault' would sound a lame excuse back in London if we had nothing to offer them – more so if 'the other side' had an extensive report.

When we at last got off the ground, there seemed no chance of arriving at the Dam on time. In fact, we landed at Aswan at precisely 11.30 – the very moment Khruschev was due to press the button for the great explosion which would send the waters of the Nile thundering along a new, man-made course. It was a 20-minute drive to the dam and as we sped along that road we listened to the ceremony on the car radio. Khruschev was speaking. We couldn't understand what he was saying; all we knew was that he had to keep on saying it for a long time if we were to have any chance of producing a film. He was a loquacious man, but to hope that he would keep talking for half an hour longer than he was supposed to was surely more than the most helpful Providence could provide. And yet, would you believe it, he was still enjoying the sound of his own voice when we arrived on the scene. Within seconds, the camera was on its tripod, the sound tapes were running – and Nat captured the finest shots of the detonation and the breathtaking, thunderous surge of the mighty waters that were to be seen later on anybody's television screen.

We returned to Cairo to fill out the story – an interview with the *Pravda* correspondent, the briefest of encounters with the

Russian leader himself, and a second-best interview with one of Nasser's Deputy Prime Ministers on the political, social and economic consequences of the Dam. We never did talk to Nasser. He would, we were told, see us tomorrow. 'Why not?' But tomorrow never came.

Nevertheless, we'd had our share of luck. As Frank and John despatched the film and tapes for the next night's programme, I set about looking for another story. My instructions from the Editor had simply been to 'pick up another two or three stories while you're in the Middle East'. I could hardly complain about lack of scope! It was refreshing, too, to be given the chance to assess the strength of current topics on the spot; situations were rarely as they seemed from reading Press cuttings back home in the office.

A conversation with the BBC's Middle East correspondent, Peter Flynn, aroused my interest in the Hejaz Railway. This was the line from Turkey through Syria, Jordan and Saudi Arabia, a wonderful engineering achievement which had been built to carry pilgrims to Mecca but which became a vital supply line for the Turks in the First World War and thus a target for Lawrence's marauding Arabs, who had largely destroyed it. Now, Peter told me, the three Arab countries had set about rebuilding the line as a joint venture – not only a physical challenge, but a fascinating political one, too. By a strange coincidence, the epic film 'Lawrence of Arabia' was showing in Cairo cinemas at the time and we all went to see it. That was enough for Nat! He couldn't wait for the opportunity to film in an area which promised such visual excitement. For *Panorama*, the 'window on the world', it seemed like a story that combined all the elements of audience appeal. We set off for Amman, the capital of Jordan and the main base for the huge enterprise.

The problems we faced there were daunting. We had no visas for either Syria or Saudi Arabia. More difficult still, Nat, Frank and John had all been to Israel to cover the Pope's visit there and had passed with him through the famous Mandelbaum Gate into the Jordanian side. The Israelis had not stamped their passports, but if their visit to Israel became known, we would be expelled from the Arab countries, if not locked up. The vast distances involved, requiring journeys deep into the desert, also stretched our resources of time and money to the limit. It was also a severe test of our ability to work together as a team in the intense heat, for long hours, sharing cramped quarters in caravans in the desert, frustrated everywhere by the local bureaucrats, hampered by illness (John had a particularly bad bout of enteritis in the middle of nowhere). Yet morale was always high, aided by a strong corporate sense of humour.

One day, in an effort to cover more ground, we split up. Nat and John went off to Saudi Arabia while Frank and I filmed in Jordan. At least, that was the plan. In fact, when Nat and John landed in Jedda, they were immediately arrested as infidels, held under armed guard and then packed off back to Amman. Another day, we all set off for Damascus by train, gambling on being allowed over the Syrian border. That paid off and our passports were duly stamped en route, but the return journey by car landed us in trouble. At the border, after our passports had been examined, we were ordered out by the Syrians and into the guardroom. 'You three have been in Israel', the officer in charge said to Nat, Frank and John. How could he know? Was he making a blind guess? They tried to bluff it out, protesting their ignorance of any knowledge about Israel. The officer angrily pointed to the faintest purple smudge in all their passports – a mark they had never noticed. At the time, there had been some public hangings in Damascus of men branded as collaborators with the Jews and feeling was running high; the situation looked black. As I appeared to be the only untainted member of the team, with no tell-tale marks to sully my passport (though I had, in fact, spent some time in Israel on a second passport), it was up to me to talk our way out of trouble. I demanded calls to the Minister of Information, the British Ambassador and anyone else I could think of. Eventually, we were all released and sent on our way back to Jordan.

Next day, back in the International Hotel in Amman, Frank and I were busy on the paperwork – labelling the rolls of film, writing out an assembly order for the film editors back home and so on – when the phone rang in my room. 'There's a Mr Paul Fox on the line from London', said the operator. 'Speak up, please, caller. Go ahead.'

'Is that you, Mike? What are you doing in Amman?'

It was a bad line, made worse by the clatter of typewriters in Paul's office in London.

'We're shooting a story about the Hejaz Railway', I told him.

'A railway, did you say? A bleeding railway? What the hell do you think you're doing, wasting your time on a story like that with a revolution going on in Cairo?'

He was furious. I was flabbergasted.

'I'm sorry, Paul, but I didn't know anything about the revolution. Communication is very difficult here. We don't get the papers until late the following day . . .'

He shouted me down. 'Call yourself a reporter? A revolution on your doorstep and you know nothing about it!'

'Don't worry,' I spluttered lamely, 'we'll get there right away.'

I put the phone down in great agitation and turned to Frank. 'There's a revolution in Cairo. Pack your bags right away. We'd better get to the airport and take the first plane out.'

I rushed along the corridor to Nat's room and banged on the door. He and John were there, checking the equipment. 'There's a revolution', I began – and they dissolved in laughter. The call had been a ruse, perpetrated by them, and I'd fallen for it completely. Nat had imitated Paul's voice from the phone in his room, speaking into a glass tumbler at some distance from the mouthpiece while John played a tape of office effects – one of several he had to practise such japes on trips like this one. It may seem a childish prank and far removed from the realm of serious current affairs reportage, yet it was as necessary as food and drink to our working together. It relieved tensions that might otherwise have developed to the point where they would have seriously impaired our working relationship. The four of use became practised practical jokers. We needed to be.

There was, however, on this trip a strange sequel. After we had finished the Hejaz Railway report, we flew off to Istanbul. From there we planned to move into Thrace to investigate reports about Turkish emigration from terror-torn Cyprus.

In my hotel room alongside the Sea of Marmara, Frank and I were doing the paperwork when the phone rang. 'There's a Mr Fox on the line from London', said the operator.

'Is that you, Mike? What are you doing in Istanbul?'

I told him about our projected visit to Thrace.

'Well, you'll have to abandon it. Mr Nehru has just died and Roderick Macfarquhar has flown out to cover the story. He'll need your crew for filming. You'd better come home.'

I'll never know why I didn't laugh and tell Nat that he couldn't get away with the same joke twice. It's as well I didn't because Mr Nehru *was* dead and that *was* Paul Fox on the line.

In the same year, 1964, I was despatched at a moment's notice to Tanganyika to cover the story of the Army mutiny there. I went on my own, with instructions to find a camera crew locally when I arrived, which seemed to me a tall order. I got to Dar es Salaam on a Thursday afternoon on the last plane in before the airport was closed to civil traffic. I had to work fast: a film would have to be flown out by Sunday at the latest if it was to be used in the next evening's *Panorama*.

The task seemed impossible. There wasn't a freelance cameraman in town and no chance of rustling one up from Salisbury or elsewhere in Southern Africa because the phones were silenced. Other crews from Britain had been and gone, following up rumours that the mutinies had spread to other Army units further north in Kenya and Uganda. Information was almost impossible to acquire. President Nyerere had apparently gone to ground, the Army weren't talking and even close friends in the Tanganyika Broadcasting Service had sealed lips. The only other person I knew in Dar was Joe Heppe, a cameraman from the American NBC network who had decided not to follow the rest of the Press corps northwards, working on the hunch that there were going to be more interesting developments where he was. He proved to be right.

Early on the Friday morning, there was the sound of gunfire coming from the sea, apparently opposite the Collito Barracks where the junior officers and men had taken over control, locking up their senior commanders. I dashed into Joe's room. He'd been roused by the gunfire, too, and was packing his gear to get out to the barracks. Could he shoot some film for me? Sorry, he had his own job to do. But I twisted his arm to lend me his second camera, a Bolex. I wasn't quite sure what I intended to do with it as I'd never aspired to more than jolly holiday snapshots with an old box Brownie. But in the car on the road to the barracks, Joe gave me some quick tips on exposure setting, focussing and resting the camera on my nose to steady the shots. At Collito, we found that the British Para-troops had dropped in from an aircraft carrier offshore. There was still sporadic shooting as the mutineers were winkled out and lined up, their arms held high, onto the barrack square. I filmed what I could and persuaded Joe to take a few shots of me among the mutineers. (The crucial difference between film and newspaper reporting is that, for television, you have to produce the evidence of being on the spot; there's no question of composing colourful copy from the comfort of a hotel room, based on phone calls and gossip.)

I suppose I only had a minute or so of film to show for my efforts, but at least it was exclusive – a scoop of a kind – and I was feeling rather pleased with myself when the Tanganyika Police arrived. Joe and I were told that we were under arrest and that we would have to surrender all our film. They were about to take us away but reluctantly agreed that we could go to the central police station in Joe's car, which carried all his equipment. I drove, with the police car following us, while Joe busily swapped films. By the time we arrived at the station, the exposed films were hidden under the seats of the car and the two cameras were loaded with unexposed film. Inside, Joe was ordered to surrender the film in the cameras, which he did while we both protested vehemently. We were held in custody for three hours – not the first time and not to be the last that I would learn how meaningless 'Commonwealth Citizenship' meant as far as basic legal rights were concerned.

When we were finally released, we made all the right noises about our confiscated film and sped to the airport, now open again. I had some valuable material in my case, but it was not enough to be in any sense a considered report. I took a plane to Nairobi and landed there in the evening with only that night and the next day left to me to produce anything of substance. With rumours abounding of a Tanganyika-style mutiny in Kenya, I questioned everybody I could at Nairobi airport and later in the New Stanley hotel that night about the threat to the stability of the comparatively new independent State. 'There is talk of trouble up country,' everybody told me, 'but as long as the Old Man is around, there's no real danger.'

The Old Man? Could they really mean Jomo Kenyatta, the man who not so long before had been branded by these same settlers and by their Governor as 'a leader unto darkness and death'? Yes, he was the man they meant, the man they had for years reviled as an instigator of the foul Mau Mau terror, the man who would surely bring about Kenya's ultimate downfall if the wretched 'liberals' gave him half a chance . . . the man who was now the country's (and the settlers') saviour. What a turn-up for the history books! There was a curious irony that here in Mau Mau land I was free to report as I pleased and to interview without restriction Mr Kenyatta down at his farm – after I had 'fled' from the country of a man in whom white friends of Africa had pinned so much faith, Dr Julius Nyerere.

My next visit to Tanganyika was even more brief and again it landed me in police custody – but this time in a different country and for different reasons. This time, in September 1964, I had flown down to South Africa to join cameraman Ernie Christie for a series of reports which took us first to Salisbury, Rhodesia, and then on to Dar es Salaam. But in Dar, Ernie (who carried a South African passport) was apprehended at the airport, declared a Prohibited Immigrant, and put back on the Comet which had brought us in. I rejoined him and we flew on to Nairobi, where we were permitted to enter the country but refused permission for Ernie to film. The anti-apartheid movement was gaining strength throughout the independent countries of Africa and Ernie, one of the best cameramen available to us anywhere in that Continent, was gradually being deprived of the opportunities to earn a living outside South Africa. (At the same time he was 'under suspicion' in his own country, whose police were none too happy about his visits to the unfriendly north.)

Ernie had no political axe to grind, of course. He was a

professional, and a very fine one at that, who had made his reputation with some brilliant coverage of the Congolese civil war, and who wanted no more than the right to work. He was being robbed of that right. The programme, I reflected, was also being robbed of a great deal of money as the two of us sat in that familiar meeting-place of globetrotting reporters, outside the New Stanley Hotel, sipping coffee or beer and wracking our brains to find some story that we would be permitted to film. On the phone, my instructions from London were to stay put, on the basis that 'something would turn up' and, I suspected, under some misapprehension about the vast distances (and therefore expense) that would be involved in our travelling to some country on this Continent which would permit a South African cameraman.

Finally, Ernie and I hit on what we thought was an ingenious idea. Stories were emanating from Rwanda-Urundi about a series of massacres there and of refugees pouring across the border, to the great embarrassment of the Uganda authorities who could not cope with their numbers. They were coming in at a point near the little township of Mbarare, which Ernie had visited once before. He knew that there was a little grass airstrip there and a small hotel run by a British couple. As there was no immigration control point, the rules were that travellers entering the country at that point were required to report to the local police station within 24 hours of their arrival. Ernie had a pilot's licence, so we decided to try flying into Mbarare, shooting our story on the border, and flying out again within the prescribed 24 hours. We hired a single-engined plane at Nairobi airport and set off on a flight which seemed to me perilous in the extreme. I had never been piloted by Ernie before and had unjustified qualms about his ability. To be sure, there were thrilling sights of rhinos, antelopes, giraffes and all the rest of the teeming wild life in the Serengeti – sights that people back home would have paid hundreds of pounds to see – and I counted the blessings of having a job which actually paid me to be there! But at the same time, I was nervous as we crossed the great expanse of Lake Victoria, my eyes fixed on that single propeller.

As we came over Mbarare, we 'buzzed' the hotel. That's to

say we swooped down low above the roof twice and then turned away towards the airstrip. 'That's the signal that we're going to land', said Ernie. 'They'll understand we want them to send a car for us.' The first car to turn up carried four Africans who silently observed our landing and then drove off without speaking to us. They might be no more than idly curious locals who happened to be passing by; they might be the so-called 'political police' who abounded in Obote's Uganda. We had no means of knowing, but at any rate we spent an uneventful night in the hotel and set off early in the morning for the resettlement camp by the border. And it was there that we were picked up, almost as though they'd been waiting for us, and taken by armed police to the town jail. The police chief was a kindly African who clearly would have been satisfied to send us back to Kenya with a reprimand, but he was under pressure from the local politicians who wanted to make capital out of our arrest. With obvious reluctance, he said that we would be tried in the magistrate's court that afternoon. There were two charges – illegally entering Uganda and spying in a prohibited area. But this did not satisfy the political commissioner and instructions were obtained from the Attorney General's office that we should be escorted to the capital, Kampala, to face trial there. We explained that we had a hired aircraft which we could not leave in Mbarare and that with Ernie, myself and our equipment aboard, there would be no room in it for any escorting policeman. That, I think, was what the police chief wanted to hear. Looking us straight in the face, he said: 'Then you will have to fly to Kampala on your own and surrender to the authorities when you land there.' We took off in the direction of Kampala, but as soon as we were out of sight of Mbarare we turned eastwards and made for Nairobi. Our gamble had failed. There was clearly no chance of any further filming in East Africa on that trip and I hopped on a VC 10 for home. The security of my own four walls was never more welcome.

By this time, I was becoming something of a jailbird – and always, oddly enough, in Commonwealth countries. My first experience had been in Montreal, filming with Erik Durschmeid the violent campaign for independence for the largely French-speaking province of Quebec. One morning, we set up the camera on a traffic island in the centre of Montreal to interview Marcel Chaput (the Republican leader who was later to become notorious for his warning that the safety of the Queen could not be guaranteed during the Royal Tour of Canada). Chaput at that time had avoided serious trouble with the authorities, though it was clear that he was under constant surveillance and that any chance to put him safely out of the way would be eagerly grasped.

We had to abandon the interview at that spot because traffic noise drowned our words, so we looked around for a quieter place – and found it on the concrete edge of the St. Lawrence Seaway, Again we set up the camera on its tripod. As we began the interview, two police cars screamed up to us. Unceremoniously we were all bundled into them and taken away to the guard house. The speed of the operation left me breathless – and baffled. What crime had we committed? There was no explanation. I demanded to speak to the British High Commissioner on the telephone but was told to shut up and shoved into a bare room along with Erik and Chaput. They kept us there for hours, allowing no communication with the outside world, and no hint of what charges, if any, might be made against us. Everyone seemed on edge – the result, I learned later, of a seamen's strike that had erupted into violence and even, in one instance, murder. In the evening, we were taken off to the city jail, put behind bars in a kind of communal cell with others who'd been picked up that night, photographed, finger-printed – and, at last, charged. 'Trespassing on Federal Government property', read the charge sheet. The case was to be heard next morning. Soon, however, Chaput's lawyer arrived on the scene, familiar no doubt with his client's being in these situations. Bail was arranged and we were released.

Next morning, we appeared in court. All the proceedings were in French. To my horror, we were charged together with 20 burly seamen and the prosecutor was demanding jail sentences for us all, without the option of a fine. Chaput's lawyer successfully pleaded that we should be tried separately and the seamen's case was heard first. They were remanded in custody for a month.

I demanded that our own case be heard in English, but this

was refused. The charge itself was translated, but nothing else. Chaput's lawyer made the peculiar plea of 'guilty with explanation' on our behalf. As the prosecutor warmed to his task, the prospects seemed bleak for us. We were adjudged guilty. But we were in luck, because the sentence was a fine for each of us of 50 dollars.

There were many more excursions and many more alarms during my foreign filming years for *Panorama* and, later, *24 Hours*. In dangerous situations I don't think I was over-endowed with courage, though I never did see the sense in ostentatious gestures of bravery by some other reporters I'd meet on my travels. I remember one morning in Cyprus, for instance, when I and just about the whole reporter corps on the island had driven into the hills, Union Jacks or white handkerchiefs fluttering from our car radio aerials, through the Greek lines and into a Turkish village that was under siege. Firing broke out from the hills surrounding the community; bullets ricocheted from the walls of houses in the village and most of us took what cover we could – except for a certain reporter from the *Daily Express* who strode out into the centre of the village square and turned to a Turk who, like the rest of us, was keeping his head down behind a substantial wall. 'Take me to your gun emplacements', demanded the reporter. It was a performance worthy of the local amateur dramatic society in *The Red Barn*. We were treated to more: 'I have a duty to my readers', he declaimed to the protesting Turks. It seemed to me then that his duty to his newspaper was to return in one piece to Nicosia, fit to file a story that would surely be dramatic enough without all his histrionics. But perhaps I was a coward.

Certainly I knew fear often enough, mostly I suppose in aircraft.

There was the Constellation whose engine went on fire as we were taking off from Tunis on our way to Accra. Full to the eyebrows in fuel it was, and we were lucky that there was no fatal explosion. Back in the safety of the airport building after we had scrambled out of those emergency exits, the airline plied us with free champagne. Cases and cases of the stuff. I have never drunk so much in my life.

There was the old Britannia of Air Cubana, kept together

with spare parts from other cannibalised aircraft, which was grossly overloaded with refugees and what they were allowed to take of their belongings from Havana. Within seconds of take-off, an engine failed and we seemed to hang perilously in the air as the plane strained to gain height and clear the mountains ahead. Even the cabin staff lapsed into a fearful silence. At Mexico City, it was the custom for immigration officials to board the Cuban planes and collect all the passengers' passports, dropping them contemptuously into sick bags and taking them away for inspection. On that flight, there were few empty sick bags left.

There was the Viscount which attempted to take off in the slush and snow at Stuttgart but failed, as ice formed on the wings, and slithered to a standstill within a few feet of the end of the runway. For perspiring moments I had visions of another disaster like that at Munich in 1958.

There was the Boeing 707 whose tyres burst as we took off from Monrovia in Liberia, and the knuckle-whitening minutes as the pilot turned to bring the plane down again.

There was that other fire, this time in a Comet almost exactly half way between Athens and Rome. 'We are returning to Athens' was all the pilot said as we spewed fuel over the sea and turned back. Most of the passengers consisted of a party of Greeks who had clearly never flown before. Their silent tension on that long haul back was terrible to see. And then, as we touched down safely in Athens, they exploded into hysterical applause. It was all so unnecessary, requiring only a few calming words from the captain and his crew, but they remained as silent (and therefore, it was to be assumed, as fearful) as their passengers.

It was on the ground, at Salisbury airport in Rhodesia, that I knew a different kind of fear. We were waiting for Ian Smith to return from negotiations with the British Government in London. There was a large crowd of his supporters there, too, ready to greet their homecoming hero. I did 'a piece to camera', commenting on the almost total lack of any opposition to the Smith régime among the white population of the country, a lack that I suggested might be politically unhealthy. As I talked, I became aware of the crowd closing in on me. I can think only of clichéd words to describe their mood – ugly and menacing. An excessively large and muscular Afrikaaner shouted, 'Lies! You people come to our country and tell nothing but lies about us. You think your Communist friends will destroy us, but we will destroy you first.' The crowd took up the angry chorus. Yes, I was frightened then. They were for all the world like a lynch mob.

And then, Smithy's plane touched down. We were saved by the bell, and by the uninhibited adulation of their leader.

CHAPTER ELEVEN

Ambitions and Obstacles

In May, 1966, I set off round the world with the over-ambitious intention of making a film series for *24 Hours* about the last outposts of the British Empire – the handful of countries still dependent, wholly or in part, on Britain. It was to be completed in six weeks. Not surprisingly, it has to be entered in the 'failure' column of my television career's profit and loss account.

I took with me two of the best operators in the business – sound recordist Ted Read and cameraman Reg Pope. Our itinerary looked rather like some pages from Bradshaw's Railway Guide, involving our hopping on and off planes in no fewer than 48 different countries: one missed connection and the whole plan could collapse like a pack of cards. It did.

The first few days augured well. We landed in Antigua (one of the Leeward Islands) by way of New York and within 36 hours had a worthwhile story 'in the can', of a little island community grappling with the problems of new-found economic and political independence but with Defence and Foreign Affairs still the responsibility of Britain. What a beautiful island it is, too! I remember one morning before breakfast when we went for a swim in one of the bays. Silver sand, languid palm trees, a crystal sea, the gentle warmth of a kindly sun. The three of us, who could boast that we had visited practically every known earthly paradise in the course of our work (yes, work!) agreed that Antigua beat the lot. I wanted so much to have the family with me, to share these delights with them. (That desire stayed with me throughout our long journey and, back home, I put the idea to Joan and the children that we should all have a holiday in Antigua. I couldn't afford it, of course – the cost for eight of us would have been in the region of £2,000 – but I was prepared to pawn my future through a never-never scheme. The proposal received a decidedly cool reception. 'We'd rather go to Holimarine in Somerset', they told me. 'There's a super swimming pool there and a playground and we make lots of friends.' So much for a father's dreams.)

From Antigua we moved on via Montego Bay to Nassau, capital of the Bahamas, tax haven, speculators' paradise, resort of rich Americans in their ludicrous Bermuda shorts and straw hats, home of the politicians at that time who were known as the Bay Street Boys and whose public political offices matched so conveniently their private commercial enterprises.

It was then that our troubles began. The plan was to fly to Miami and on to Mexico City, Acapulco, Fiji, and then the British and French condominium of the New Hebrides – the most vital link in our complicated logistic chain, because there was only a weekly plane service on that leg. The chain broke in Acapulco. On landing there, a fault was found in our aircraft's radio equipment. We were taken into town for an unscheduled overnight stay which in the end lasted for three long, frustrating days. Time after time we would be put on a bus to go to the airport; time after time another fault would develop in the aircraft and we would be transported back to town. As the hours and then the days went by, frustration grew to anger among the passengers and one evening in the airport departure lounge I thought there was going to be a riot. Our equipment was still aboard the plane because we were officially 'in transit', but this was clearly a scene worth filming, even if it had nothing to do with our brief. I asked Reg to try to get permission to unload the camera so that we could shoot a sequence there, and off he went with a Mexican immigration official.

A few minutes later there was the sound of some rumpus going on behind the scenes and the Qantas station manager came up to me: 'Your colleague is in serious trouble. He has hit one of the Mexicans who wouldn't let him unload his gear.' Reg emerged, protesting that he had merely given the man a friendly slap on the back. 'That may be so,' the Quantas man told me, 'but he has been reported to the police. I will do what

I can to smooth things over, but please be careful during the rest of your stay here because you will certainly be closely watched.' I knew what he meant. Previous experience of Mexico had made me only too aware of the police penchant for locking people up and asking questions later. Much later. There was a real danger that our own frayed tempers could lead to our reporting assignment coming to an abrupt end.

'We'll have to be exceptionally careful', I said to Reg and Ted. 'Whatever happens, don't argue with any of the officials as long as we're here. Refer them to me.'

It was a pompous thing to say and Reg reacted to it. Back at the hotel yet again, we sat down to dinner and he turned to me: 'Leader, will you ask the waiter if I may have a glass of water? Leader, may I have a plate of soup?' He was joking, but it was a rather sour joke and it gave notice that those delicate relationships which were so vital to the success of a working trip like this were under severe strain. However, the tension was greatly eased when that plane at long last got off the ground and headed across the Pacific for Fiji: champagne was called for, and music, and we danced with our fellow passengers up there at 30,000 feet.

But the pack of cards had collapsed. From Fiji I rang my editor, Derrick Amoore in London, and told him of our troubles which included missing the flight to the New Hebrides. He mimicked my plaintive voice. 'How awful! Three days stuck on the beach at Acapulco. With all that hot sun, too. It must have been hell. Our hearts bleed for you.'

Australia. A precious day spent with my brother Roger, who had made this truly a 'land of opportunity' by making a fortune as a farmer there. More Australian than the Aussies themselves by now. He called me a 'wingeing Pom', mainly it seemed because I was unimpressed by 'his' fountain at King's Cross in Sydney.

The teeming life of Hong Kong, surely the most exciting city in the world.

A flea-ridden bed in Bombay.

A night spent under armed guard at Johannesburg airport, where we were refused entry because foreign correspondents were banned during the visit of Robert Kennedy.

Mauritius, where I upset the French. Interviewed on

television and asked the usual question about 'what do you think of our island?' I was indiscreet enough to remark on the paternalism of the sugar plantation owners, the racial discrimination, the poverty of the Creole population. Next day, at the racetrack in Port Louis, our attempts to film were drowned by boos.

Swaziland and another frightening flight with Ernie Christie when we got lost in the clouds between the mountain-tops.

Rome. Tangier. Gibraltar.

Home, exhausted and disappointed with a series of film reports which, for a whole catalogue of reasons (or excuses) were no better than second-rate.

Put it down to experience.

CHAPTER TWELVE
Window on My World

THE BASIC TECHNIQUES of television today are familiar to most people. What were once regarded as wondrous triumphs of science are now accepted as commonplace. When men travel to the Moon we expect to see and hear them there – in colour, naturally. Nobody is surprised, or even excited, any more to be accosted in the street by a film team seeking his views on issues of the day. 'Audience participation' is the fashionable phrase and output on all channels abounds with phone-ins of one sort or another.

And yet, despite the familiarity of it all, all manner of myths persist about the men and the making of television. People like me are imagined to be a kind of expense-account jet set, hugely paid, glamorously pampered, probably neurotic. It is said that we can manipulate, and therefore misuse, this powerful medium for our own ends (whatever they may be). We can, it is supposed, utilise our professional expertise to bully our 'victims' when we interview them.

Let us examine these illusions.

What is the purpose of an interview? It is to inform, to entertain and to educate the viewer. The three aims are, as Stanley Unwin would have it, 'intertwingled'. The most educative of programmes will fail if it is so unentertaining as to send the viewer to sleep, or to an alternative.

There are basic skills in asking questions: preface them with a 'why?' or a 'how?' and the danger is avoided of a mono-syllabic 'yes' or 'no' answer. Listen. An interview should flow like a conversation, with questions arising logically from answers. Remember that the viewer has not had the advantage of access to research material on the subject under discussion;

Interviewing showbiz personalities is not normally my cup of tea. I can never think of anything remotely interesting to ask them and squirm at the prospect of plugging their latest film, or play or musical tour.
But Zsa Zsa Gabor . . . now that was something different. She pulled out all the stops and there was a grave risk of my committing indecent assault in front of ten million people.
Is she the world's most exciting woman?

framing questions which show that an interviewer 'knows his subject' will irritate more viewers than it impresses.

These and others like them are the simplest of rules. Their aim is not to place the interviewer at some 'advantage' (as though his job were to score rhetorical points, which it isn't), but to elicit information as effectively as possible. Contrary to common belief, any opportunity to manipulate the facts is in the hands of the person being interviewed.

Let me give you an example. Following questions in the Commons some years ago about private arms dealing, I phoned a retired army officer who was known to be in the business. Let us call him Captain X.

'Yes,' he told me in answer to my enquiries, 'I sell large quantities of arms abroad. And I'm not ashamed of it. Don't you go calling me a Merchant of Death or any of that newspaper rubbish.'

'To whom do you sell these arms?'

'To anyone who wants to buy them, of course. We're doing a particularly good trade in the Congo at the moment.'

'Which side?'

'To both sides, of course. That's no concern of mine. I'm in the business to make money like anyone else.'

'And the Yemen?'

'Yes, that's a particularly good area just now. Both the Royalists and the Republicans. Very good customers they are. As a matter of fact, we have a big order for Lee Enfield rifles going out there soon.'

'Would you be prepared to come on the programme and tell us about your business?'

'Certainly. I'm proud of it.'

And he did appear. The interview went something like this:

'Captain X, I understand you sell quantities of arms abroad. Can you tell me where they go?'

'Yes, the Belgians are perhaps our best customers. We've sent some big orders to France, too.'

'Anywhere else? The Congo, for example, or the Yemen?'

'Good gracious, no, I wouldn't do that. It would be most improper.'

What was I to do, knowing that he was lying? I tried again:

'Captain X, I am bound to say that this is not what you told me when we spoke on the telephone earlier. You made it quite clear then that you carried on extensive business with factions in both the Congo and the Yemen'.

Blandly, he replied, 'No, no, you clearly misunderstood me.'

Even in retrospect, I can think of no so-called 'professional technique' which could have elicited the truth that night. If anybody manipulated that interview, it wasn't me!

Similarly, the television reporter is hampered by the laws of libel – properly so in cases where the reputation of the innocent ought to be protected, but contrary to the public interest when (increasingly nowadays) those laws are used to prevent the exposure of criminal activities.

In 1965, I set out to investigate an alleged protection racket in London's East End, said to involve the notorious Kray Twins, Ronald and Reginald. By phone, I made contact with Reggie, who agreed to talk to me provided I went to see him alone, without cameras or colleagues. He said that I should be at the entrance to a certain underground station at seven the following evening.

I arrived on time, to be met by a huge black man who led me into a nearby pub. And there, sitting alone at a table with not another customer on the premises, was Reggie. I was given a seat opposite him and the waiter brought us drinks as we talked, while the black man sat silently at another table across the room.

Reggie Kray talked to me at length, particularly about his charity work in the East End and the many celebrities who had helped him and his brother with their fund-raising activities. He showed me photographs of the twins in their dinner jackets, posing with the stars. He had a naive pride in them, like some schoolboy with an autograph book. When I asked him about stories of intimidation in the pubs and clubs of the vicinity, he dismissed them as nonsense. Moreover, he suggested that I should see for myself by visiting a selection of premises with a camera the following evening. The selection was made by him.

In the first pub we visited the next night, the manager told me, 'There is no protection here and no trouble. I do not even know the Krays'. As he talked, I spotted our black friend at the end of the bar. We moved to another. 'There is no protection . . .' The form of words was precisely the same, and the black man had moved in ahead of us. The pattern was repeated in every establishment we visited that night. It was convincing evidence that all the managers and proprietors took their orders from Kray under the eye of his henchman – convincing to me, that is, but not the sort of evidence that would substantiate a television report.

Later, when our equipment had been packed away and the black man had gone home, I was taken into the private room of a club proprietor. 'Of course there is a protection racket', he told me. 'Only it goes under cover of charity. Every week, the Krays' men come to me for a donation of £25.' He paid by cheque – made out to a well-known personality who was said to be a trustee of the charity. My informant was, not surprisingly, too frightened to confirm this information in a public interview and the long days and nights of work we put into that investigation never materialised as a programme item. The laws of libel saw to that. Even today, with the Krays securely in jail, there is no possibility of naming other names.

The political interview is a quite different kettle of fish. Yet again, far from allowing the interviewer to manipulate the medium and his 'victim', the converse can so easily be true.

'Minister, why has the government failed to halt inflation?'

'Before I answer that, Michael, let me just say a word or two about our achievements in the battle to improve our environment . . .'

What am I to do? Interrupt him and demand that he answer my question rather than treat us to a party political? If I do, there will be complaints that I am rude, aggressive, bullying even. If I hear him out, I shall be accused of 'letting him off the hook' and allowing him to use the programme as a party platform. All I can say is that my own inclination is towards the former approach.

And, outside the studio, how good is 'the good life'? The posh restaurants. The plush hotels. The fast cars. The fat cheques. Another myth.

I enjoy eating out with Joan or with close friends (who are more likely to be countrymen than 'personalities') in restaurants not too far from home, preferably where it is not necessary to wear a jacket and tie. Cod and chips, out of paper, is my delight. Its only rival is roast lamb at home for Sunday lunch. Exclusive restaurants in town are places I would happily exclude from my life. I visit them only to work, as convenient meeting places in the course of programme research, where I nibble at the tarted-up food I abhor.

Hotels are lonely resting-places in the course of working journeys; cars take me to and from work; cheques may be fat but they are largely illusory. The Inland Revenue has a hefty stake in them and they will only keep coming in as long as my face fits the square-shaped screen, as long as somebody somewhere regards me as a marketable commodity. If mine is an average career in television, that will not be for long.

What a joyless paragraph that seems to be, now that I come to re-read it! In truth, my work gives me an intense pleasure that I am unable to analyse but deeply grateful for. It is my window on a world not so much of places and things but of people and ideas.

A world I want to share.